9-85

Date Due

| NOV 0 3 1988 | | MAR 3 0 |
| AR 1 6 1991 | | MAY 0 1 |

Helping
Children of Divorce

A Handbook for Parents and Teachers

SUSAN ARNSBERG DIAMOND

SCHOCKEN BOOKS · New York

To Ace and Adrienne, Bert and Rose

First published by Schocken Books 1985
10 9 8 7 6 5 4 3 2 1   85 86 87 88
Copyright © 1985 Susan Arnsberg Diamond
All rights reserved

Library of Congress Cataloging in Publication Data
Diamond, Susan Arnsberg.
   Helping children of divorce.
   1. Children of divorced parents—United States.
2. Home and school—United States.   3. Parent-teacher
relationships.   I. Title.
HQ777.5.D53   1985   306.8′9   84–22191

Designed by Nancy Dale Muldoon
Manufactured in the United States of America
ISBN 0–8052–3974–X

Grateful acknowledgment is extended to Ann Landers and News American Syndi-
cate for permission to reprint the letter on p. 62 which originally appeared in the
Ann Landers column.

While actual quotes and examples have been used throughout this book, names
and/or dates have been changed to provide anonymity.

Communications to Divorced or Separated Parents

The Schools shall develop and maintain such communications with divorced or separated parents as may be in the best interests of the child or children involved. To that end, provided that the School District has not been given a legally binding document specifically removing the parent's right to have knowledge about, and participate in, his or her child's educational process, the following guidelines shall be observed:

1. In keeping with the U.S. Family Educational Rights and Privacy Act, both custodial and noncustodial parents shall, upon request, be given full access to their children's school records, and shall also be granted all other rights provided by that Act.

2. Upon written request from custodial or noncustodial parents, noncustodial parents shall be sent such written communications as are commonly sent to custodial parents (e.g., report cards, notices of parent-teacher conferences, notices of "open house" meetings, etc.), provided that they pay any unusual costs involved (such as the costs of duplicating extra material or mailing material beyond the regular mailing area).

3. Teachers and other professional personnel shall attempt to conduct parent-teacher conferences with both custodial and noncustodial parents if such conferences are requested. Such confer-

ences may be held separately or with the two parents jointly. The primary concern shall be to establish effective communication concerning the child.

4. The schools shall make reasonable efforts to inform both custodial and noncustodial parents of their rights under this policy.

Policy Adopted: 1/11/82
Board of Education

Contents

Acknowledgments

THE NATURE of the counseling relationship implies confidentiality; therefore, it is not possible for me to mention the full names of the many young people whose experiences have enriched this book. Nevertheless, with a caseload exceeding 250 students a year, I know anonymity is preserved if I use first names. So, my first thank you goes to the kids (in many cases more than one kid with the same name): Adam, Ann, Billy, Chris, Debbie, Diane, Eddie, Gary, Greg, Gretchen, Jane, June, Karen, Kim, Leslie, Lisa, Marcie, Nancy, Noreen, Pam, Pat, Patti, Rich, Robbie, Steve, Tim, and Wendy.

The following adults also gave invaluable help: Richard Gardner, Gerald Giges, Arnold Hodas, Saul Kapel, and William Lewit, psychiatrists who gave of their time to answer my questions and review some of my writing; Richard Brill, Esq., Lawrence Brown, Esq., and Aaron Weitz, Esq., who gave me a background in divorce, law, and schools; Paul Glick, retired senior demographer, Bureau of the Census, and V. Jeffery Evans, Health Science Administrator, Demographic and Behavioral Sciences Branch, Center for Population Research, National Institute of Child Health and Human Development, who made available and clarified data on divorce and changing family structures; and Elinor Dicker, Education Specialist for the Mental Health Association of Westchester, whose encouragement came at the right time.

It is impossible to thank all of the school personnel, clergy, and parents who allowed me into their offices, their homes, their lives—

but I do want to mention Nancy Krim, Lynda Mandlawitz, and Harriet Sobol, who gave most generously of themselves whenever needed.

And finally my thanks go to my husband, Bob. His journalism background proved invaluable and his willingness to accommodate the haphazard home schedule of a working high school counselor, who was at the same time writing a book, made this book possible.

Introduction

ONE SPRING morning seven years ago, Mr. Smothers phoned me from New York City. He had just arrived from the West Coast and was on a business trip, he said. He was hoping to come up to the high school to find out how his son, Joey, was doing. Mr. Smothers was a divorced, noncustodial parent. I knew Joey well and also knew that he was doing nicely in school, so I saw no reason why I should not share this information with his father. But during the hours that passed before Mr. Smothers' arrival, I wondered about my responsibility to this man. I also wondered about my responsibility to his son, Joey, and to Joey's mother. Further, and more troubling, I wondered what I would have said to Mr. Smothers if Joey had not been doing well.

As I spoke to colleagues in the following weeks, I came to a realization. There were many questions, but not many answers, when it came to dealing with a family who had divorced. There was, in those days, no literature aimed at helping school personnel to understand and to work more effectively with parents and children experiencing separation and divorce.

In fifteen years as a high school counselor I have watched the divorce rate rise dramatically. I have also watched fathers take a more active role when they don't have custody. I have watched working mothers who have custody juggle schedules to attend a school event. And I have been keenly aware that school personnel have expressed a desire to respond better to children and parents experiencing separation and divorce. Still, general, practical advice for school personnel has been lacking.

The school is clearly in a position to make a positive contribution. After all, school may be the only consistent factor in a child's life at this time and teachers should be in a unique position to provide support and some guidance. In most instances, teachers have daily contact with their students—six to seven hours a day, five days a week. At the minimum one-fourth of a child's day is spent in school. To make the most effective use of their capabilities, teachers must obviously understand the needs of their students. And students experiencing separation and divorce often have special needs.

I was asked by Doris Breslow of the Scarsdale Teachers Institute to develop a course to acquaint teachers with the implications of divorce. In conjunction with this effort, I began interviewing divorced parents and my counselees from single-parent homes. Parents and children alike were eager to share experiences and feelings, and offer suggestions as to ways in which school personnel could better meet their needs. Indeed, there was more to be learned than I had anticipated. I requested time to expand my research on ways in which schools could work more effectively with parents and children experiencing separation and divorce and was subsequently awarded a Professional Development Leave by the Scarsdale School District.

This effort, then, represents the culmination of my research and fifteen years of experience. I have interviewed separated and divorced parents (in custodial, noncustodial, and joint-custody arrangements), children, matrimonial lawyers, psychiatrists, clergy, social workers, and the following school personnel: principals, psychologists, librarians, nurses, secretaries, and teachers. Initially I had one goal—to develop a practical guide that would enable school personnel to help children whose families were experiencing separation and divorce. As this book neared completion, however, and was shared with divorced parents, there was unanimous agreement: this book would be equally helpful to separated and divorced parents with school-age children. Therefore, I direct the information in this book to two groups: to divorced parents whose children attend elementary and secondary schools and to the school professionals who work with these children and with their parents.

Susan A. Diamond
Dean of Students
Scarsdale High School
Scarsdale, New York

Helping Children of Divorce

1

The Facts

NINETEEN seventy-five was a sociologically significant year: the number of American marriages ending in divorce
topped the million mark for the first time in history. In fact, between 1965 and 1975 the divorce rate more than doubled, leading
Americans to worry about a divorce epidemic. The number of divorces granted in the United States continued to rise in the seventies: 1,090,000 in 1977, 1,130,000 in 1978, and 1,181,000 in
1979.[1] Although divorces have declined somewhat in the eighties
(1,180,000 in 1982; 1,179,000 in 1983), the number remains great.
And behind each statistic is the dissolution of a family, with all the
emotions and adjustments attendant upon such a transition.

A majority of these families include children, who must come to
terms with the fact that divorce is an adult decision over which they
have no control. More than 1.5 million children under the age of
eighteen are affected each year by family breakups. Findings from a
National Survey of Children, sponsored by the Foundation for
Child Development, indicate that in 1976 over 25 percent of children ages seven through eleven did not live with both biological
parents. The survey further revealed that 77 percent of the children
not living with both biological parents were from families with
incomes of less than $5,000. Only 16 percent of the children not
living with both parents were from families with incomes of over
$25,000. Thus, contrary to popular belief, divorce is not most

---

1. These figures from the National Center for Health Statistics do not include
divorces obtained by Americans outside of the United States.

prevalent among the wealthy; it is much more prevalent at the lower end of the economic ladder. This study found that income and education are closely intertwined with marital stability: the more education and income, the more stable the family.[2]

Data on Harvard graduates seems to corroborate the comparatively lower divorce rate among the privileged. Statistics gathered for the *Twenty-fifth Anniversary Report,* compiled for each class's twenty-fifth reunion, show the following: By the time of their twenty-fifth reunion in 1979, 17 percent of the class of 1954 had been divorced. In 1980, 19 percent of the class of 1955 had been divorced. In 1982 data for Princeton, Yale, and Harvard were presented in the *Twenty-fifth Anniversary Report.* Current marital status was reported, in part, as follows:

	Princeton	Yale	Harvard
Married, first time	72%	67%	72%
Remarried	9%	11%	10%
Divorced	5%	7%	5%

The road to divorce was smoothed considerably in the 1970s as many sectors of society began to recognize divorce as an acceptable alternative to an unhappy marriage. Whereas testimony casting specific kinds of blame on one's spouse used to be required before a divorce would be granted, many states have expanded the grounds for divorce to include vaguer grounds or have adopted groundless statutes. For example, no-fault divorce allows a marriage to terminate without blame and is in effect in at least ten states. In twenty-one states separation for a period of from six to twenty-four months (depending on the state) constitutes grounds for divorce.

When couples say, "We have separated," there are three possible interpretations. For one, it can mean that two people are no longer

2. Nicholas Zill, "Divorce, Marital Conflict, and the Mental Health of Children: Findings from the National Survey of Children," presented at the Children and Divorce Symposium, sponsored by Wheelock College, Boston, Mass., November 1978.

living together. It's a physical condition only at that time, although it may have legal ramifications later.

The other interpretations do carry legal standing. They are technically called legal separations. "We are separated" in one legal sense means that a lawsuit has been filed in court for a separation decree. Legal separation, enacted through a separation decree, is obtained by people who, for one reason or another, don't want a divorce. These people live apart as single, but are not free to remarry.

A second type of legal separation is obtained by people wishing to divorce and perhaps remarry. These people may obtain a legal separation that entails a separation agreement signed by both parties. Custody, visitation rights, alimony, child support, health care provisions, and division of property are among the items included in a separation agreement. In many states this kind of legal separation becomes the grounds for divorce.

If children are involved, custody is an integral part of the separation agreement. When divorce follows a legal separation, the separation agreement usually becomes part of the divorce decree. In the absence of a separation agreement, custody is specified in the separation decree or divorce decree.

"Custody" is the assumption by a parent of the responsibility for the day-to-day decisions affecting the health, education, and welfare of the child. It is estimated that custody is not contested in 80 to 90 percent of divorce cases. In most cases, custody is granted to the mother; in fact, nine out of ten custodial parents are mothers. The noncustodial parent is often, however, interested and involved.

The concept of joint custody was introduced in the seventies and has gained support in the eighties. The mother and father share equally in the responsibility for the child, each parent having equal rights in decisionmaking and spending time with the child. In joint-custody arrangements, the parents often live close enough to each other so that the children can conveniently continue to attend the same school no matter which parent they stay with. The late seventies also found more fathers requesting, and being granted, custody of their children, and this arrangement has also gained support in the eighties. Although the people involved in these latter arrangements are still proportionately few, their numbers are growing. Thus, children of divorce may live only with their father, only with their mother, or with each parent alternately—a fact that people who work with children need to recognize.

A change in custody is difficult to effect; nevertheless, a parent can, at any time, make application through the courts for a custody change. Technically, children are in the custody of a parent until the age of eighteen. Yet in most states the court does pay attention to the custody preferences of children once they enter their teens.

Children may not change their last name after the divorce—to that of a stepfather, for example—unless there is a legal adoption or a legal name change through the courts. Some families prefer that everyone under their roof has the same surname, and their children summarily change last names. Without court approval, however, this is not legal.

The question of which parent's name should appear on school documents is often confusing. This is understandable. School personnel do not always ask the appropriate questions, parents do not always volunteer the answers, and school forms are often not structured to include information about parents who are living apart. Legally, unless there is a court order to the contrary, the noncustodial parent is still a parent and is entitled to recognition as such by the school. (Stepparents, although they may be interested in their stepchildren, have no legal standing.) The noncustodial parent's name should be included on school documents whenever the name of "parents" is asked for.

Under the U.S. Family Educational Rights and Privacy Act, the noncustodial parent is entitled to information regarding school achievement and progress whenever he or she requests it (unless there is a legally binding document specifically removing the noncustodial parent's right to have knowledge about the child's educational process). Suggestions for revision of school forms to include appropriate information on the noncustodial parent and suggestions for sharing school information with both parents are presented in chapter 11.

When an emergency arises, the noncustodial parent has the second legal priority to be contacted, unless there is a court order to the contrary. The person with first priority is, of course, the custodial parent. In some cases, noncustodial parents live a great distance from their children or their whereabouts are unknown. So it is possible that they would be of less help than neighbors or close relatives. Indeed, the custodial parent often lists these people on school forms as the ones to be contacted should an emergency arise. No one, however, has the legal right to act in an emergency unless designated by both the father and the mother. It would seem appropriate that when children are living with both parents, both parental signatures endorse the person to contact in an emergency. These signatures could be obtained as part of the initial registration procedure.

Kidnapping is a source of concern for school administrators as well as for parents. Although the school has the legal responsibility for children from the time they come to school until they leave at the end of the school day, single parents especially may wonder about the measures a school takes to protect their children. Principal Parker Damon has quoted one concerned single parent as follows: "I wish I had more confidence in the school not releasing my child to the wrong person."[3]

It is of utmost importance that school officials specify guidelines for releasing children to anyone other than custodial parents or legal guardians. These guidelines should be regularly reviewed with both the professional and nonprofessional school staff. Knowing to whom a child can be legally released during the school day is as important for secretaries and teacher's aides as it is for teachers, administrators, or the school nurse.

3. Parker Damon, "When the Family Comes Apart: What Schools Can Do," *National Elementary Principal*, October 1979, p. 72.

2

Informing the School
of Separation and Divorce

> When you go through a divorce, you know you're
> different. You don't have as much money, you
> have to change houses, give up your bedroom, et
> cetera. In the beginning you don't want to talk
> about it. You just want to get through it.
>
> *Mother of three, five months after her divorce*

PARENTAL emotions at the time of separation or divorce range from relief that a bad relationship is over to severe depression. Some parents contact the school without hesitation; some are so absorbed in their problems that it takes a tremendous effort for them to make the contact; others never make contact.[1] Since most parents present a stiff upper lip to outsiders, school personnel need to be aware of the kinds of feelings that may be operating when a newly separated or divorced parent contacts the school:

Failure: "I couldn't make my marriage work."

Shame: "There's a stigma attached to being divorced—there's a strike against the children."

---

1. Judith Wallerstein reported that in the Children of Divorce Project, a longitudinal study of 131 normal children's reactions to their parents' separation and divorce begun in 1970, half of the children's teachers didn't know about the divorce. This was reported in response to a question at the Children and Divorce Symposium, Boston, Mass., November 1978.

Guilt: "I'm very sad that I've had to put my children through this. I feel guilty about the child for not having given him the best I could give him."

Insecurity: "I had no identity. When the 'Mrs.' came away, I collapsed."

Sensitivity: "Unsolicited advice is awful."

Parents may contact the school strictly to impart information, or they may come for support or guidance. To respond appropriately to these parents is obviously important, for it establishes a relationship that can effectively serve the child's best interests, and subsequently those of the parent and of the school.

In general, the ideal initial response from school personnel is one of nonjudgmental caring. The school should convey the feeling that it cares about what's happening to the child but is not making judgments. There is important information about the child's home situation that the school needs to know:

1. When did the separation/divorce occur?
2. When did the parents tell the child?
3. Has the father/mother left? When? Where did he/she go? Should the school have his/her phone number? Address?
4. Does the father/mother visit regularly?
5. Do both parents want to be informed about school progress and/or functions such as Open House?
6. What is the school's responsibility to the noncustodial parent if he/she contacts the school? What about emergencies?
7. Are there any other changes in the home situation?

If the separation or divorce has recently occurred, the parent may understandably be very sensitive. These are tender times. If a parent contacts the principal, counselor, or classroom teacher, he or she no doubt wants to inform the school of the change in the home situation so that a school professional will be alert to—and understanding of—the child's behavior. The school professional should not try to elicit any more information than the parent comfortably offers at this time, but would do well to lay the groundwork for a meeting in the near future. Making specific arrangements for the parent to phone or come for a meeting to discuss how the child is handling things and how the school might help is essential. Not only will making these arrangements convey caring to the parent, but the meeting or telephone conversation will give the school professional an opportunity to ask the questions listed on the preceding page.

It is not improper for the school professional to impart a feeling of confidence by saying, "We've been through this before," or "We have many other children in the same situation." The custodial parent is usually alone in dealing with the child at first. "The aloneness is the worst part of it," explained one parent. A statement such as suggested above will help the parent to feel that there is someone with experience who understands the situation and can help share a bit of the burden if need be.

At the second conference, or when meeting with any parent whose separation or divorce is not fresh (as in the case of a parent registering a child in a new school), the aforementioned questions should be asked. It is wise to let the parent know why questions are being asked. The teacher or administrator might say something like: "If you wouldn't mind answering a few questions, it would help me to understand your child's situation better." It might also be helpful, depending on the circumstances, to request a copy of the custody segment of the legal document. This would clarify the school's responsibility to each parent. Because many women have stated that they are especially sensitive after the separation or divorce and resent being asked if they are going to work ("Aren't three kids legitimate work?" questioned one mother), the seventh question is intended to elicit that information without being offensive.

The school professional can also ask whether the parent wants the information kept private; whether it should be disseminated to teachers; or whether the teachers should be first contacted, asked how the child is doing, and then informed of the separation or divorce.

Often the parent will ask to be notified if the child begins to have problems. Parents stress that they want to know that the teacher will be on the *lookout* for problems, but will not *look for* problems. One of the main reasons custodial parents hesitate to contact the school after a separation is the fear that the teacher will then look for problems. (Another reason is the parent's concern that the child will be treated as "different.")

If the parent has asked for notification of the child's progress, or has asked to be contacted if the teacher observes any changes or problems, the school professional has an obligation to let the parent know as soon as the information is available. It is legitimate for the parent to assume that all is going well if not informed to the contrary. The burden of communication lies with the school professional.

Finally, conveying availability to the parent—"If there's anything happening that you think I should be aware of, do contact me," or a sincerely spoken "Keep in touch"—will further impart this feeling of support and nonjudgmental caring.

The issue of divorce is a new one to school personnel, and teachers and administrators may be unprepared for some of the circumstances that arise. They have gone into the teaching profession because they like children and they like to teach. They may, however, be unfamiliar with special techniques for responding to adults in crisis. It is understandable that they may respond in ways that seem correct to them but are nevertheless professionally inappropriate. Common mistakes are giving unsolicited advice, making judgments, sharing personal experiences, and being overly sympathetic.

The mistake of judging and offering well-meaning but unsolicited advice is demonstrated by the experience of Mrs. Lesoe. When she and her husband separated, she had two children in school, one in first grade, the other in third grade. She had been very active in the PTA and knew many teachers on a first-name basis. When she told the third-grade teacher that her husband had moved out and they were separated, the teacher responded that "the baby [the third-grader] wasn't ready yet" and said she didn't think they should divorce now.[2] Mrs. Lesoe felt defensive. She came to impart infor-

---

2. Psychiatrists often identify the Oedipal (ages three to five) and adolescent periods as those periods in which children are most likely to be negatively affected by divorce, but there is by no means unanimous agreement. Dr. Richard Gardner, in *The Parents' Book about Divorce*, states: "I am not convinced that there are particular periods during which the child is especially vulnerable to the effects of parental separation. Rather, I believe that from the day of birth the child needs both parents

mation, not receive advice. She recalls that she was trying to look interested and remain polite while "basically ignoring what was said." At that moment she resented the unsolicited advice and mentally tuned out.

When Mrs. Lesoe informed the first-grade teacher, the teacher listened, then suggested that the parent look into Masters and Johnson's *Human Sexual Response*. This suggestion may have been one of those inappropriate things people say when they feel uncomfortable, or it may demonstrate a lack of sensitivity or simply be another case of unsolicited advice. Mrs. Lesoe, five years later, is still not sure how to interpret that comment. She *is* certain that it made her uncomfortable.

Mrs. Fox, on the other hand, received no unsolicited advice. She had known Miss Williams, her son's nursery school teacher, for many years. When Mrs. Fox informed Miss Williams about her separation, Miss Williams broke down and cried. Mrs. Fox found herself in the position of having to console the teacher, telling her not to worry, that things would work out. She changed roles, in effect, with the teacher. In looking back, Mrs. Fox observes that the teacher responded empathically, not objectively, as a friend, not as a professional. But Mrs. Fox went to the school with the expectation that the teacher would respond professionally. The teacher misinterpreted her role in this instance.

Sometimes a teacher may try to be supportive by sharing miseries or taking the parent's side, as Mrs. Hensen experienced. Mrs. Hensen, a working mother, did not notify the school immediately. She waited until the parents' conference night at the school the next month. Her daughter's second-grade teacher was young, attractive, and single. Upon hearing of Mrs. Hensen's recent separation, the teacher responded by telling Mrs. Hensen how upset *she* was with

---

and the removal of either is likely to have harmful effects on his or her psychological development. . . . The only generalization with regard to this matter that I do believe to be true is that the younger the child is when the loss occurs and the longer he is exposed to the loss, the greater will be the harmful effects" (New York: Doubleday, 1977, pp. 43, 44).

Mr. Hensen's behavior, and she recounted some of her personal experiences. The teacher was trying to tell Mrs. Hensen, "I'm on your side; I understand." But Mrs. Hensen did not want to hear anyone else's experiences, nor did she want the teacher taking her side. She did not need or want that kind of relationship from the school. She recalls that she was flabbergasted at the teacher's unprofessional response and decided that she could expect no help from such a naive, immature teacher. Therefore, she shared no further information with the school.

Any response from the school professional that causes the parent to feel defensive, uncomfortable, or overburdened will result in that parent's inability to give the school the kind of information it needs to work for the best interests of the child. When divorced or separated parents make the initial contact, they are not necessarily looking for support, comfort, or therapy. Therefore, one shouldn't pass judgment, make jokes, or give advice unless the parent has asked for it. Should a parent come for advice, referral to the school counselor, social worker, or school psychologist may be appropriate. It is also appropriate to make the parent aware of the PTA, community, and local and national support groups (see page 95). Parents who contact the school, no matter what the relationship or circumstances, expect the staff to respond with the objectivity of professionals.

3
Placing the Child
in the Classroom

It was a lonely, big place [the high school]. I was
really scared. I made one friend that year and ate
my lunches in the bathroom. I felt if I never came
to school, the only person who would have known
would have been the attendance clerk.

Sixteen-year-old girl reflecting on her freshman year.
She had moved to a new town with her divorced
mother two days before school began.

THERE are two natural opportunities to manipu-
late the child's school environment so that it can more positively
affect his or her well-being. The first presents itself when a divorced
parent moves and the child enters a new school. The second presents itself at the beginning of every school year.

Not infrequently, a change of residence and consequently of
schools follows divorce. When this happens it is but one of a multitude of changes with which the child must contend. "My children
left behind their friends, their school, their home, their father, and
their dog," explained one divorced mother, who had returned to
the town she'd grown up in. How, then, can this particular change
be made less painful—or even beneficial—for the child of divorce?

Psychological literature documents the importance of youngsters
having appropriate role models with whom to identify as they grow

up. Boys are influenced by their father's actions and behavior in ways that enable them to develop male attributes; likewise girls are influenced by their mothers. Further, studies find that many boys in single-parent families who lose their fathers before age five show greater identification with females in the preschool and elementary school years. This is not a permanent condition but may affect their relationships with others throughout their lives. Boys and girls who grow up with both father and mother tend to develop an easier relationship with members of the opposite sex. As Richard Gardner points out, "The boy's relationship with his mother and the girl's with her father serve as models for future relationships with the opposite sex."[1] It is understandable, then, that a single parent might well request that his or her child be placed with a teacher of the same sex as the parent who has left the home. Such a request might be more common at the elementary school level, where the majority of each day is spent with the classroom teacher.[2]

At least 90 percent of the parents who have custody are mothers. It can thus be assumed that in most instances a mother would be requesting a male classroom teacher for her children. In the 1980–81 school year one elementary school teacher in six (or 16.9 percent) was male.[3] In a given class, children whose parents have divorced comprise anywhere from less than 1 percent to over 50 percent. It would therefore appear difficult to honor all the requests for male teachers. In addition, a class taught by a male teacher and composed primarily of children from single-parent families would lack the advantages that a heterogeneous group provides. How, then, does the school respond to a divorced mother's request for a male teacher? How do school administrators answer the mother who states, "My kids, as far as I'm concerned, couldn't have enough male figures. A strong male figure is good and should be available"?

1. Richard A. Gardner, *The Parents' Book about Divorce*, p. 160.
2. Such a request might not be true at the secondary level, for if the father left and the adolescent felt anger at the father, this anger could be directed at male teachers and could cause difficulty.
3. *Digest of Education Statistics*, U.S. Dept. of Education, National Center for Education Statistics, 1982, p. 52.

The school and the parent must determine whether the sex of the teacher or the personal qualities of the teacher should have priority. And this can best be done by focusing on the needs of the particular child. If, for example, a young boy is experiencing sex-role confusion (e.g., if he begins to dress like a girl), a strong case can be made for a male teacher. Otherwise, psychiatrists think that the teacher's personal qualities are a major influence in shaping the child's classroom experience and should be given priority over the teacher's gender. Further, if a child has a regular, ongoing relationship with the father or has other adult male family members, there are role models available. What personal qualities, then, characterize the teacher who can best serve the needs of children of divorce?

A teacher who is *consistent* in classroom routines, expectations, and behavior can bring some sense of order to a youngster's life following separation and divorce. This is important because home routines have often broken down during this period. Dr. Robert Weiss found that parents experience disorganization, depression, unmanageable restlessness, and a chaotic search for escape from distress in the eight to twelve months after separation.[4] If coping is difficult for the custodial parent and if family routines have been disrupted, a teacher who is consistent, who helps to make the child's world more orderly, can make a very positive contribution to that child's life.

The need for consistency must not, however, be confused with rigid structure or inflexibility. Being *flexible*, in fact, is a very important quality in a teacher, for it is probable that the youngster will run into some problems during the period of separation, divorce, and readjustment, and a flexible teacher can help to ease the pressure during these times.

The teacher who is *alert* and *responsive* can be particularly helpful by contacting the parent if unusual behavior is observed. That teacher may be the first to observe unusual behavior or may call attention to something the parent noticed but did not consider significant. Before the divorce there was a partner with whom the par-

4. Robert S. Weiss, *Marital Separation* (New York: Basic Books, 1975), p. 236.

ent could share concerns about the child. Now, in most cases, the parent must rely on his or her own observations and judgments. Single parents have the sole responsibility for parenting. They are Johnny-on-the-spot twenty-four hours a day, and they say it's tiring. If, following divorce, the mother goes out to work, she has even less time and energy for parenting while she tries to cope with and balance a myriad of demands. The alert teacher can be an accurate observer of unusual behavior. It is appropriate to report this behavior to the parent in terms of observations rather than judgments. (For example, "Mrs. Jones, I've noticed in the last two weeks that when Susie comes to school she has dark circles under her eyes, yawns a great deal, and puts her head down on the desk and closes her eyes" is preferable to "Susie seems very tired. I wonder if she's getting enough sleep.") When a child's problems seem serious, explaining the role of the school psychologist, social worker, and counselor and helping the parent to contact one of them is appropriate.

Parents also say that when teachers contact them to let them know that all is well with their child, they are most appreciative. The fact that someone at school is looking out for their child is a welcome source of support.

Since the child may feel deprived of affection, attention, and/or time with his or her parent, a teacher who can fill some of these voids—who is *caring, patient, attentive,* and *understanding*—can also be a valuable support. Stated one working mother with a six-year-old son: "If I were doing it over again, I would look for— no, I would insist on—an understanding, supportive, motherly teacher."

It is easy to identify caring and supportive teachers. Nevertheless, teachers may consciously or subconsciously give more support to girls than to boys. At least one study, at the University of Virginia, has found that our cultural bias toward expecting males to cope and not show emotion operates in the nursery school setting. It leads one to wonder if this is true also in the primary grades and, indeed, throughout school. Analysis of this study showed that the same kind of whiny, clinging behavior exhibited by little boys and litle girls received different responses from the same nursery school teacher. For example, when a little boy would come up to the teacher and cling or try to pull on her skirt, she would say, "Go away, don't do that." But when a little girl exhibited the same behavior, the teacher would say, "Stop doing that," and then pick the little girl up and put her on her knee.[5] Support is equally necessary for all children at this time, and teachers who consider themselves caring and supportive might do well to analyze their responses to boys and to girls.

High school students emphasize the importance of understanding and caring in a teacher, but their definition of caring includes setting limits. Teenagers say that when a teacher shows understanding, students feel support and usually want to make an effort in that class. However, if the teacher doesn't also care enough to set limits, members of this age group say they are inclined to manipulate and could continually use the divorce as an excuse. Their suggestions about the ideal personal qualities that a teacher should have are sensitivity, understanding, and caring enough to set realistic expectations for the student.

Another consideration when placing the child in the classroom is whether or not the teacher is divorced. Several parents of elementary school youngsters were grateful for the sensitivity shown to their children by divorced teachers. "One of my son's teachers was superb," recalled a divorced mother of a nine-year-old. "She was young, had been divorced, and at appropriate times told the pupils straight out how kids and adults feel at that time. My son came home and was pleased that he had a teacher who cared and understood." Another mother shared these feelings: "My daughter's teacher was a divorced, custodial parent herself, and I just knew that the teacher was sensitive," she said. A recently divorced psychologist commented, "I don't know whether the school's placing my son with a teacher who was divorced was purposeful, but it was helpful."

5. E. Mavis Hetherington, "The Effects of Divorce on the Social and Cognitive Development of Children," presented at the Children and Divorce Symposium sponsored by Wheelock College, Boston, Mass., November 1978.

Psychiatrists confirm the value of exploring this kind of placement. Here is the rationale: if the teacher has gone through divorce and has handled it well, this should provide a positive experience for the child. The child observes a parental figure who has been successful in coping with divorce, and can see that the teacher has "made it" and that divorce is not a stigma. Further, if the child likes the teacher, it may help to reduce the resentment that children often feel toward their parents for divorcing. Put simply, the child can see that nice people, like the teacher, get divorced and can handle it. (Obviously, where any teacher is bitter, not coping, or lacks the personal qualities previously mentioned, placement would be inappropriate.)

A few parents noted that their children had been placed in elementary school classes where there were other children from divorced families. In one case, the two children in a particular class became close friends. In another case, a divorced mother and her third-grade son were talking one night when he explained how different he felt. *His* parents were divorced. The mother had noticed on the class list that there were other children with a single parent listed, and there were children whose last names differed from their mother's. She pointed this out to her son. Just knowing he wasn't the only one made a difference, she said.

A second-grade teacher remarked that two girls in her class had become good friends. Both had divorced parents. One girl was bright and able, and had parents who were amicable. The other girl had experienced a bitter divorce, was of average ability, and clearly exhibited pain as a result of the divorce. The second girl was able to draw upon the first girl's strengths and made significant gains, both academically and personally, during the year. Although the friendship was not the sole factor in her success, the teacher feels it played a significant part.

The commonality of divorce is a plus when children in the class have learned how to cope with this situation and can help other children to work out similar problems. It can be a negative experience, however, if two problem-ridden or withdrawn youngsters gravitate toward each other and isolate themselves from the rest of the class. In such instances, an alert and skillful teacher would be wise to intervene.

There are, then, options to explore when placing the child of divorce in the classroom: sex of the teacher, personal qualities of the teacher, marital status of the teacher, and the possibility of other children from divorced families being in the class. These options can be presented to the parent of the child entering a new school, or to the parent of a child who would seem to benefit from them when the new shool year begins. Above all, it must be remembered that each child is a unique individual with his or her own personality and needs. And this is where a skillful and sensitive school professional can help the parent to assess the child's needs in determining proper classroom placement.

At the junior and senior high school level, where there are often different teachers for different subjects, the administrator or counselor should discuss options and priorities with both the parent and the adolescent. A positive school experience five days a week, thirty-six weeks a year, is certainly worth the thought, effort, and time involved in planning the best possible placement.

4

The Effects of Separation and Divorce

My parents, after twenty years of supposed "wedded bliss," told my brother, sister, and me that they were "not happy with each other" and that the children were not to blame for it. We had no guilt feelings; however, we were mildly in shock. How could we have been so naive, so unsuspecting?

Since my parents separated, I have experienced several uncomfortable situations ranging from silent evenings with my father to tearful moments with my mother. My brother and sister have been asking me questions, many of which I do not have answers to.

The night my parents told us, I only felt comfort with my dog. I spent the entire evening holding him in my arms and sobbing into his furry neck. He was so good. It was as if he understood. He has been the most helpful of everyone since this whole mess began. *Sixteen-year-old girl*

"WHAT should I look for, and how can I help?" is a common response from teachers who have learned of separation or divorce in a student's family. To answer the first part of this question, one must know that the child will typically have certain psychological reactions to separation and divorce. Sadness or depression, denial, embarrassment, anger, guilt, concern about being cared for, regression, maturity, and somatic (physical) symptoms are common reactions.

Some of the initial reactions to divorce are similar to the reactions to the death of a loved one. This is not surprising when one realizes that the family, as the child knew it and grew up in it, has died. In contrast to death, however, the two parents live on, and their presence—or absence—continues to be a factor in the child's development.

All of the research indicates, and all of the experts agree, that divorce is a very painful transition in the lives of most families who go through it. In the Children of Divorce Project, all 131 children (ages two and one-half to eighteen) initially found the transition acutely painful. Even in families where fighting and abuse had openly taken place, preadolescent youngsters failed to see divorce as a logical solution and felt their parents should stay together.[1] If their parents fight, all parents fight, they reasoned. For adolescents, divorce may be seen as a relief in some instances; most of the time, however, there is pain.

If divorce is so painful, why do some children flourish academically? Why do others sound mature and logical when explaining their family situation? Why do others carry on as if nothing has happened?

The reactions a child exhibits will depend on the nature of the child (ego strength and capacity to mobilize resources), as well as his or her age and the relationship of the parents and child before, during, and after the divorce.

---

1. Judith S. Wallerstein and Joan B. Kelly report in "The Effects of Parental Divorce: Experiences of the Child in Later Latency," *American Journal of Orthopsychiatry* 46, no. 2 (April 1976): ". . . most of these children [ages nine and ten] were unable at the time of the initial counseling to see any justification for the parental decision to divorce. . . . Although one father had held his wife on the floor and put bobbie pins in her nose while the two children cried and begged him to stop, both children initially strongly opposed their mother's decision to divorce" (p. 261).

SADNESS OR DEPRESSION: Sadness almost always exists initially and should be considered normal unless it continues for months. Primary-grade youngsters do not have the skills to verbalize their feelings and most likely will say something like "I feel sad" to account for a host of mystifying, unpleasant feelings. The Wallerstein-Kelly study found that pervasive sadness affected six-, seven- and eight-year-olds who seemed to have few ways available to deal with their sadness.[2]

In general, youngsters may look forlorn. They may feel fatigued, and the fatigue may slow them down and affect their decisionmaking. They may feel "down" and fail to find satisfaction in any of the activities they used to consider fun; they may withdraw from their friends and drift off into daydreams; they may easily burst into tears; they may have difficulty concentrating. On the other hand, for some children, school may provide a haven where—for a time—they can escape their feelings of sadness. They tend to throw themselves into activities and academics; they will most likely achieve well. To their teachers, these youngsters will look as if they are having no problems.

Depression, on the other hand, is more extreme. It involves a lackluster, drained, hopeless, helpless, empty feeling. When youngsters feel depressed, their eating habits often change, and they usually find it hard to concentrate in school. They may not have the discipline to make themselves do assignments or, at the secondary level, go to class. A teenager describes depression: "When depressed, I'm very quiet, withdrawn, unhappy. I feel like crying, I'm very temperamental, and I really hate it when people say 'What's wrong?' or 'Are you OK?' And I feel like nobody cares."

DENIAL: A common psychological mechanism for testing but not accepting the reality of a loss is denial. It also provides insulation from feelings that may be acutely painful or situations that are

2. Judith S. Wallerstein, "The Impact of Divorce on Children," presented at a workshop sponsored by the Center for Preventive Psychiatry, White Plains, New York, December 1976.

overwhelmingly dangerous. The denial mechanism works without the person's being aware of it. Parents, for example, are often stunned when their children say that the separation has come as a complete shock. This is especially true when heated arguments or strong disagreements have openly taken place in front of the children. As one mother communicated to her son's high school counselor, "Jason experienced a severe emotional upheaval last year when his father and I separated. This took place in January, and hard as it was for us to believe, it came as an enormous shock to Jason and our other sons. . . . It was not until midsummer that he began to be himself again."

The psychological mechanism of denial is powerful and unconscious and can prevent one from seeing the obvious. To deny separation or divorce in the early stages is not uncommon. The denial takes place because of the fear of acute pain.

There is another kind of denial. This denial is conscious and stems from the hope that if the divorce is not discussed, the parents might change their minds. A final reason for denying the separation or divorce is embarrassment.

EMBARRASSMENT: A feeling of embarrassment may last for years in children of divorce. Nobody likes to be different, and although we are very aware in the 1980s that a significant number of families have divorced, when it's happening to a particular child, that child feels different and sensitive, and is vulnerable to the loss of self-esteem that manifests itself in embarrassment. A ninth-grader whose parents had divorced seven years before cautions, "If you have to mention it [the divorce], mention it to the student when no one's around." Embarrassment is a common reaction in all children. It's one of the primary reactions to which teachers must be sensitive.

ANGER: Another very common and natural response for children to feel when the marriage breaks up is anger. When one realizes that an integral part of their lives—their family—will no longer exist as they knew it, and that their sense of security and well-being is threatened, anger is certainly understandable.

As opposed to younger children who don't like to show anger toward either parent, the Wallerstein-Kelly study found that intense anger was the central response for nine- to twelve-year-olds. "The scaffolding of their life was collapsing, but they figured the best defense is a good offense," stated Judith Wallerstein, who noted that the anger ran its course in a year if it wasn't fueled by the parents.[3] Children may feel anger toward the parent they believe responsible for the divorce or anger at being made different from their peers who live with both parents. They may feel angry that the remaining parent doesn't have enough time for them, demands too much of them, and so on. A high school senior confided that she felt angry that *she* didn't matter, while her divorced parents quarreled over how much money each would or could give toward her college education. "The money and their feud seemed to count more than me, more than my education, and that really hurt me. We're put in second place—after the money, after the new wife, after the feuds," she said.

Admittedly there are good reasons for these angry feelings, and being able to express them openly is healthy. Unfortunately, children can't always do this, and the anger may be disguised in other forms.

GUILT: One of these disguises is guilt—a form of anger directed unconsciously at oneself. Guilt is seen in children of all ages when their families separate. Although it has been stated that children often feel guilty for having in some way caused the divorce (when they haven't), the Wallerstein-Kelly study found that this kind of guilt was not prevalent.

A common cause of guilt in children is the loyalty conflict. Most children have been raised to feel love and a sense of commitment to both of their parents. So when parents separate, children often find themselves feeling self-conscious and sensitive about their relationships with both parents.

This feeling was articulated by a high school sophomore whose

3. Ibid.

parents were living in the same house until the legal separation was finalized. That morning he had come to school feeling so guilty that he'd cut all of his classes. "I just can't say goodbye to them in the same room," he confided. "I've got to say goodbye to my dad and goodbye to my mom in separate rooms. It's uncomfortable—I feel as though I'm doing something I shouldn't do in front of the other—I mean kiss my mother goodbye and shake my father's hand."

CONCERN ABOUT BEING CARED FOR: The child's concern about being cared for manifests itself in various ways. Commonly it is seen in elementary school children as a fear of abandonment, and in adolescents as worry over who will pay for material things such as college. Elementary school children worry that if their father could leave them, could their mother also leave them? Or, if their mother could stop loving their father, could she stop loving them also? They experience an increased sense of vulnerability, especially to the possibility of the death of the custodial parent. They may develop anxieties about being separated from the custodial parent and try to resist going to school, lessons, or even parties. Some may steal meaningless items in an effort to make up for lost security.

For some teenagers, the concern over college financing is so distressing that they've rearranged demanding academic programs to make time for a job, even when it's not necessary. After rearranging one senior girl's schedule to enable her to work in the afternoon, the guidance counselor received the following note: "The college interviewers told me that my light load of senior year classes would jeopardize my chances of getting in. Therefore, I decided to add on to my schedule and not get a job. To eliminate the problem of finances, I decided that I would take the money out of the bank, which has been put aside for me from stocks, grandparents, etc." Money is a prime source of friction between ex-spouses, and insecurity about it is very threatening to teenagers. It may affect their school program, their school performance, and their psychological well-being—even in affluent families.

REGRESSION: People of any age may regress as a result of an experience that shakes their security. Regression reflects an inhibition about going on to the next stage and may freeze people where they are or take them back to an earlier stage they remember as being secure. In the school-age child, it may be evidenced by an increased dependency on the teacher. Clinging, whining, and looking for laps to sit on are common manifestations of this behavior in primary-grade children. Older children may seek to establish personal contact with the teacher again and again, perhaps by asking for continual reassurance. They may feel incapable of working independently or following directions and may solicit the teacher's help repeatedly.

MATURITY: On the other hand, maturity may blossom in youngsters because of the additional responsibilities they must assume. In single-parent households, each person is integral to the functioning of the household. Thus, children not only assume adult tasks but are often treated like adults by the custodial parent, who, in fact, depends on their help and solicits their advice. This may lead to the child's feeling set apart from his peers with two parents at home, for they may seem frivolous by comparison in their day-to-day concerns. Teachers value maturity in their students, but it must be weighed against the effects of a curtailed childhood.

SOMATIC SYMPTOMS: In the elementary school, somatic (physical) symptoms tend to consist primarily of stomachaches and headaches, although other aches are also reported. Six- to eight-year-olds seem to have more tears connected with their aches and are more emotional, observes an elementary school nurse. She suggests this is because they perceive the home problems through their "emotional antennae" but are unable to verbalize their feelings.

Wallerstein and Kelly report of nine-, ten-, and eleven-year-olds that "one symptomatic response observed in this group, and not seen in any younger group, was the report of a variety of somatic symptoms of different kinds and degrees of severity, such as headaches and stomachaches, which the children related to the parental conflict and the parental visits."[4] (These may be especially obvious on Fridays and Mondays and around vacation time.) The school nurse reports that when nine- to eleven-year-olds come to her with aches, their tears are restrained and there is a certain quietness to their demeanor, as contrasted with younger children.

Adolescents complain of fatigue and headaches and nervous stomachs. In all cases there is the need to touch base with a nurturing figure when youngsters come to the nurse's office. And they need to be assured that their symptoms are taken seriously.

The responses discussed above are normal and are frequently seen in children whose parents have separated. Precisely which ones the child exhibits depend on many factors. What school professionals need to understand is that children normally react to stress in time frames that last from a few days to a few months. If the reactions have not disappeared after two months, there is strong reason to believe that the child cannot come to terms with his or her problems alone and that professional help—through the school psychologist or an outside professional—is indicated. Remember, a reaction does not have to be dramatic to be considered abnormal. Some of the mild reactions, like daydreaming, may not be as apparent as daily temper tantrums, but if the daydreaming lasts too long, it becomes abnormal. An abnormal reaction may not always be a matter of intensity; it may in fact be a matter of duration. And this is where there is no substitute for an alert and responsive teacher.

The preceding pages have answered the teacher's question "What should I look for?" The following chapters will address the question "How can I help?"

4. Wallerstein and Kelly, "The Effects of Parental Divorce," *American Journal of Orthopsychiatry* 46, no. 2 (April 1976): 264–265.

5

Sensitizing Teachers to the Nontraditional Family

As I stand here writing these words in my father's room I ask myself these questions:

What is it like to live with a mother and father at the same time?

What is it like to have both parents to help when there are problems?

What is it like to have both parents live in the same part of the country and at least be able to talk to your mother on the phone without it costing a fortune?

WHAT IS IT LIKE?

Maybe the person who reads this will have the good luck of having both parents together and appreciate what it is like. *Nine-year-old boy*

THROUGH both general and specific behavior and activities, teachers are in an important position to help students touched by separation and divorce. Without special effort they can effectively serve as good role models, as discussed in chapter 3. A special, conscious effort may be necessary, however, if teachers are to develop a sensitivity to the nontraditional family.

In 1979 the Census Bureau estimated that 45 to 50 percent of children born in the 1970s would live in a single-parent family

before they reached the age of eighteen. Of these children, an estimated 32 percent would live with a divorced parent. (The others
would have a parent who is widowed, separated, never married, or
married but living away from home.)[1] These children of the 1970s
comprise the student population of the 1980s. If present trends
continue, 40 percent of the children born in 1983 will experience
parental divorce and 20 percent will experience a second divorce,
according to census reports.

Many children, then, will not only experience a parental divorce,
but will experience the remarriage of one or both parents and will
have to adjust to stepparents and perhaps to stepbrothers, stepsis-
ters, half brothers, and half sisters.[2] Teachers should be aware that
all of their pupils don't necessarily live with their mothers and
fathers. And the teacher's ability to apply this awareness to everyday classroom situations is even more essential. It has the immediate value of creating a more accepting and comfortable atmosphere
for children living in an alternate family situation. It has the future
value of legitimizing differences for children, some of whose parents may separate or divorce at a later date.

Since separation, divorce, and nontraditional family arrangements are undisputably more commonplace today, many people
have concluded that children do not feel as embarrassed or as different as they did in previous decades; these people may assume
that children do not need special attention unless they are having,
or causing, problems. While one cannot dispute the statistics, one
can take issue with the conclusion. As discussed in the last chapter,
the feeling of embarrassment can last for many years. Remember
the advice given by the ninth-grader: "If you have to mention it [the

1. Paul C. Glick, "Children of Divorced Parents in Demographic Perspective,"
Journal of Social Issues 35, no. 4 (1979): 176.
2. "Most remarried men have children from their prior marriage, and two-thirds
of remarriages experienced by children involve a previously married man," according to Larry Bumpass, "Demographic Perspectives on the Consequences for Children of Changing Marital Patterns," (The Demographic and Behavioral Sciences
Branch Center for Population Research, National Institute of Child Health and
Human Development, National Institutes of Health), May 1983, *Final Report*, no.
1-HD-02852, chap. 2, p. 9.

divorce], mention it to the student when no one's around." His parents had been divorced seven years earlier, and he had been part of a happily remarried two-parent family for six years. A tenth-grader whose parents had worked out a joint-custody arrangement recalled: "We were writing our class schedule on a form for Open House, and I knew each of my parents would come separately and would need a copy of my schedule. But I wouldn't ask the teacher for two forms." The attitude reflected by these statements reveals the sensitivity that young people feel when their parents have divorced. Regardless of present circumstances, they don't want to be singled out as different. Thus, by the way they view the family unit, teachers are in a unique position to maximize or minimize the everyday reminders that these children are different. When teachers recognize that many children do not live with both natural parents, and when they speak and act accordingly, they create a more comfortable atmosphere for their students. The students will, in turn, respect teachers more, for they will not have to make allowances for the insensitivity that is unwittingly displayed by the uninformed, unaware teacher.

The following suggestions are intended to achieve two goals: (1) to make teachers more aware of and comfortable with students in nontraditional families and (2) to prevent situations that are embarrassing for parents, students, and teachers.

1. ASSUME THAT SOME OF YOUR STUDENTS ARE NOT LIVING WITH BOTH NATURAL PARENTS. THEN IDENTIFY THOSE STUDENTS.

This sounds logical and simple; yet many schools do not provide teachers with this information. All that is needed is an accurate class list, with the parents' names entered along with the student's name. If there is a divorce and the custodial parent has not remarried, "Mrs. Ann Jones, Mr. Charles Jones" is appropriate. If remarriage has taken place, "Mrs. Ann Carnegie, Mr. Charles Jones" would be appropriate, opposite the name of their child, Jeff Jones. Let's look at what happened when Jeff entered Mrs. Pollock's fourth-grade class.

Ann (Mrs. Charles) Jones had remarried in June and became Mrs. Carnegie. The Carnegies had moved into their new house at the end of August and were delighted to learn that their next-door neighbor's son, Austin, would be in Jeff's class. Austin offered to walk to school with Jeff on the first day and take him to class. Austin felt grown-up with this responsibility, and the Carnegies were happy that Jeff had made a new friend so quickly. When the two boys entered Mrs. Pollock's classroom, Austin introduced Jeff to Mrs. Pollock as "Jeff Carnegie." Jeff was flustered and before he could explain the mixup in last names, Mrs. Pollock had checked her class list and declared that he was in the wrong class. There was no "Jeff Carnegie" on her list. Austin couldn't understand what he'd done wrong, Jeff was upset, and some uncomfortable moments passed before Mrs. Pollock understood the situation.

The initial confusion and embarrassment for all could have easily been avoided if the teacher had been given a class list that included the parents' names. True, some schools maintain that they have difficulty obtaining this kind of family information and therefore have problems compiling an accurate class list of this kind. If schools follow the suggestions for the revision of school forms offered in chapter 11, this information should be readily available, unless the parent intentionally wishes to hide it.

2. GET THE NAMES RIGHT.

This requires making a special effort to know the mother's last name if she has remarried. Equally important is calling the stepfather by his own surname (not his stepchild's) if he should visit the school. Stepfathers who visit their stepchild's school say they are usually making a special effort to be involved, and when teachers address them by the name of their wife's *ex-husband,* they feel awkward at the very least. Stepfathers say they make no attempt to correct the teacher in these instances; instead they make allowances.

Getting the names right is also important when acknowledging relationships to the student. The stepfather should not be called the father; he isn't. And this unthinking mistake on the part of the teacher may contribute to the child's thinking that his real father is a "nobody." (Obviously the same theory holds true for children with stepmothers.) Using the name that the child calls the stepparent acknowledges the relationship. If in doubt, ask the student how to refer to the stepparent. When teachers don't distinguish family relationships correctly, the students will make allowances; they rarely, if ever, correct the teacher.

3. MAKE IT EASY WHEN WRITTEN COMMUNICATIONS OR GIFTS ARE TO BE SENT HOME.

Christmas, Mother's Day, Father's Day, Open House—any occasion that calls for written communication to, or gifts for, parents may pose an awkward situation for the child in a nontraditional family. Indeed it is difficult to know just how to best handle these occasions. One mother happily commented that her daughter's fourth-grade teacher was sensitive to the recent divorce and arranged for the child to make two gifts for Christmas, to write two invitations to Open House, and so forth. The daughter gloomily commented, "I'm the only one who had to write it twice." Thus, the problem becomes one of allowing exceptions without making them obvious.

After asking children and their parents how to reconcile this problem, there seemed to be agreement on the following approach: when there are letters or forms that should go to both separated parents, it might be wise to put the forms on a table and let the youngsters come up and take as many as they need. The tenth-grade boy who was filling out the Open House schedule form, for example, said he wouldn't ask the teacher for an extra form even if the teacher was distributing them personally to each student. If the forms were lying on a table, however, and he was allowed to take as many as he needed, he said he wouldn't have hesitated to take two forms. (After all, he reasoned, some kids take two forms because they're afraid they'll mess up the first one.)

Sometimes the teacher can see that filling out certain forms will present problems for students in nontraditional families. At these times it is advisable to say something like, "If there are parts you aren't sure about, leave them blank and I'll check individually with you later."

When occasions call for the making of gifts, Mother's Day gifts, for example, can be made for mothers or grandmothers or aunts or any woman who is special to the child. The same holds true for Father's Day gifts and for Christmas presents. Offering options is important and valid.

4. AVOID EMBARRASSING QUESTIONS.

This sounds like obvious common sense. Nevertheless, there are some ordinary kinds of questions that don't seem embarrassing but can be. For example, questions pertaining to family may well cause embarrassment to youngsters who don't live in the traditional two-parent family. In addition, if there is a "problem" parent—a parent who ran off with a lover, an alcoholic parent, a parent in jail, a parent who's out of work—family questions can be even more difficult for children.

Colleen Wright, a teenager whose alcoholic father left the family five years ago and whose mother, a senior executive, is living with a man, cautions, "Asking 'What do your parents do?' is like asking you to tell your life-style. It's too personal."

5. RESPECT CONFIDENTIALITY.

The confidentiality referred to here concerns details of the student's family structure. A student's family situation should not be divulged to others without permission.

"After recovering from the initial shock of my parents' divorce," recalls sixteen-year-old Ann, "my main concern was keeping my friends and teachers from knowing. I remember begging my mother not to tell one of her closest friends because she had a daughter my age (eleven). I was afraid that if people knew, they would feel sorry for me and look upon me as something different." Ann's mother did tell Ann's teacher, however. This teacher had taught Ann's older brother and knew the family somewhat, and Ann liked him. Ann remembers that it was reassuring to go to school the next day and know that the teacher would understand if she should feel bad. This initial feeling of reassurance turned to distrust and anger a few weeks later, however. It seems that a new student had tried to become a member of Ann's group of friends and had been rejected. When the new student shared with the teacher her hurt at being rejected, the teacher disclosed Ann's family situation as a reason for Ann's unfriendly attitude. When Ann learned of this disclosure, she felt betrayed. "Not only did that destroy my trust in my teacher, but it also destroyed all the reassurance my mother had been giving me that the divorce would not be discussed with people outside of our close friends." Ann says that from then on, she hated the teacher.

Parents who inform the school at the time of separation and divorce usually do so because they want understanding and support for their children. Some tell their children that they are informing the school; others do not. Some want the teacher to let the children know that they are aware of the situation; others do not. It is a good idea to ask the parents how to handle this information.

It should be noted that teenagers say it is sometimes confusing when they believe that someone has informed their teachers, but the teachers make no attempt to acknowledge this to the student. They then wonder if perhaps the teachers weren't informed; or if perhaps the teachers were informed, but feel too awkward to acknowledge it. A simple "Your mother/father/counselor spoke to me, and if I can help, just let me know" is sufficient.

6. RECOGNIZE THAT CERTAIN CLASS PROJECTS MAY CAUSE EMBAR-
   RASSMENT; THEN TAKE ADVANTAGE OF OPPORTUNITIES TO LEGIT-
   IMIZE DIFFERENCES.

In the primary grades, where one of the early units may be learn-ing about the family and another unit may be studying occupations, there are many potential sources of embarrassment for children whose families deviate from what is considered the norm. It is difficult, for example, for children to know how to respond to questions about mothers and fathers they have not seen in a long time. It may be hard to draw a family tree when the child has an extended family. And it is even harder to respond to the teacher's amazed "I didn't know you had so many brothers and sisters!"

The imaginative teacher can, however, make these early units constructive and interesting by legitimizing differences. A study of the family might include, for example, a comparison of families in other cultures where men have many wives or women have many husbands. Instead of asking children to tell specifically about their father's or mother's job, the sensitive teacher can say something like, "Think of an important man or woman in your life and tell us about his or her job." In this way the class learns about the job, while the teacher finds out whom the youngster considers important. Since some children's names differ from their mothers' (if the mothers have remarried or have resumed or retained their maiden names), a discussion of names and their origins could prove interesting and informative. Asking "Whose name do you have?" or "What was your grandmother's name?" or "What was your grandfather's name?" could provide the basis for an educational discussion leading to increased sensitivity about the whole issue of names.

7. At Open House and similar events, expect from one to four parents.

Traditionally, Open House is a time when parents and teachers have an opportunity to meet and discuss the child. It should be expected that separated and divorced parents may come alone, together, or accompanied by a new husband, wife, or friend. Sometimes four parents appear on behalf of one child. Parents comment that they sometimes sense a certain awkwardness on the teacher's part, especially when divorced parents attend these occasions together. "If the divorced parents aren't uncomfortable attending a school event together, certainly the teacher shouldn't be uncomfortable," declared one divorced mother.

8. MAINTAIN AN OPEN MIND REGARDING THE WORTH OF
SINGLE-PARENT FAMILIES.

Parents of elementary school children in particular express criticism of teachers for maintaining what the parents perceive as a narrow, traditional view of what the family should be. While this criticism may result from the single parent's own insecurities and doubts about providing all of the necessary ingredients of a "good" family, it may also be fostered by a teacher's insensitivity to the seven areas just cited.

True, the stresses of separation and divorce are difficult for all family members at first, and neither the family nor its members function optimally at this time. Yet research suggests that in the long run parents should not stay in a conflicted marriage for the sake of their children. Studies by Hetherington and Wallerstein indicate that two to three years after a divorce, most children in single-parent families function better than children in two-parent families experiencing marital discord. (The research also concludes that boys are more vulnerable to the stresses of divorce and take longer to readjust.)

Although everyone is in agreement that living in a happy two-parent family is the ideal situation for children, the need for teachers to be sensitive to and nonjudgmental of nontraditional families is clearly evident. To effectively develop objectivity and sensitivity, however, teachers must assess their own attitudes and feelings about the family. Personal biases are inevitable; but once teachers realize what their own biases are, they are in a better position to remain objective and not look for problems or place blame simply because divorce or separation has occurred. With a sensitivity to the eight areas cited and with an awareness of their own attitudes, teachers are much better equipped to work constructively with students and their parents in single-parent and nontraditional families.

6

Helping Students through the Crisis: The Role of the Teacher

ALONE

Who will understand me?
Snobbishly I feel my peers are
Naive.

They feel no inner feeling,
No contemplation of what life
Means for them in eve.

They know not of pain,
Rejection, abandonment which
I have held for years.

Often I want to scream in
Their tic-toc ears.

I wish my childhood would
Have lasted for a few more years.

Eleven-year-old boy

THERE are general, as opposed to specific, ways that teachers can help the student whose parents have separated or divorced. In addition to developing and exhibiting a sensitivity to nontraditional family arrangements, teachers can create a support-

ive environment in their classrooms and can, if desired, establish a
significant personal relationship with the student.

The child experiencing the crisis of parental separation needs, at
every grade level, to make sense out of this situation. He (or she)
needs to be able to air his feelings without being judged. He needs
someone he can count on, someone who will recognize his feelings
and give him a sense of worth. He needs someone to set limits when
appropriate, someone who will be a friend, an adviser, or a surrogate parent if need be. He needs someone to help him learn to cope.
For the classroom teacher to fulfill all of these needs would be a tall
order. But since children spend at least one-fourth of their day in
school, and since school may be the only consistent factor in a
child's life, let us look at ways that teachers can make a unique
contribution.

The atmosphere that teachers create in their classrooms is important, for it can encourage openness and respect and provide opportunities for children to share feelings without being judged. As
pointed out in chapter 4, it is normal for children going through
separation and divorce to experience emotional reactions. Further,
it is healthy for children to express these emotions, which, if re-
pressed, usually come out in disguised and often maladaptive
forms. For this reason, the classroom where feelings can be safely
shared is of special value to a child experiencing a crisis. A teacher
need not be psychologically trained or even psychologically oriented to provide this kind of classroom atmosphere. "We have a
family feeling of caring for each other," states a successful teacher.
"I say to my second-graders, 'You take care of each other because
we're in this together.' " By teaching her students to look out for
and care about each other, she is making it safe for them to express
ideas, opinions, and feelings without fear of ridicule. Admittedly,
this kind of classroom atmosphere is more easily achieved in the
elementary grades, where the teacher spends a greater proportion
of time with the same children each day. Yet many imaginative and
sensitive secondary teachers achieve this feeling of community in
their classes.

A teacher who has little or no psychological background may wonder how to respond to the feelings a youngster expresses in class. *To respond properly is simply to recognize and acknowledge whatever the child is feeling.* For example, if a child tearfully says, "I couldn't sleep last night because my father left and my mother was very upset," the response "Yes, it must be hard to sleep when something upsetting happens" acknowledges the feeling. If, on the other hand, the child shares something personal and the teacher ignores it, the child will wonder why. He may think that the teacher can't discuss it because it's frightening, worthless, embarrassing, or even too terrible to talk about. It is therefore of paramount importance that teachers respond to the feelings their students share with them and the class. In a classroom where the teacher acknowledges and legitimizes the worthiness of a child's feelings, two things are accomplished: the child is enabled to express emotions he might otherwise repress, and he is given the feeling that what he is thinking and saying is worthwhile.

Too often our natural inclination is to think that to be helpful we must give children an opinion or offer a solution. When this happens, it is well to draw upon the experience of a counselor who helped elementary school teachers work with children from divorced families through a specially funded program in the Mill Valley, California, schools. "Generally, in a group, children won't talk about anything they can't handle," observes this counselor. "But if a child does seem to be in a lot of psychological pain, it's OK. The teacher does not have to rescue the child." When a teacher observes that a student is experiencing great psychological pain, the school psychologist and guidance counselor should be informed immediately. And although this may be an uncomfortable experience for the teacher, it must be remembered that if the child had not had the opportunity to express these emotions, they probably would have gone unnoticed and led to more serious consequences.

There are teachers who would like a more personal, one-to-one relationship with their students but are insecure about handling such a relationship properly. Psychiatrists suggest that when a child seeks out a teacher to talk with, the teacher must have certain qualities that caused the child to seek him or her out in the first place. So basically the teacher can trust his or her instincts when responding to the youngster.

"I think teachers can be encouraged to follow their instincts," states a minister who is highly regarded by young people in Scarsdale, New York. "I remember when I was counseling the dying in a New York City hospital and I told the supervising chaplain that I'd been operating on my instincts and now I'd like to read about it. He told me, 'When it comes down to it, you can trust your basic instincts and that's what you will use. If it doesn't work, try something else.' I think teachers can do more than they think they can."

Teachers worry that if they say something and it isn't right, they may do damage. Professionals suggest this is usually not the case unless a child is very distressed or "fragile," as they put it. "There's a large latitude for error," explained one psychiatrist. "But the more fragile the child, the less latitude there is." The majority of students who seek out the teacher are not so fragile that an inappropriate comment from the teacher will cause a tragedy. So trusting instincts and allowing for spontaneity tempered with prudence are generally appropriate. The following suggestions, however, serve as good guidelines for teachers who want to help children as effectively as they can.

GIVING ADVICE: Teachers should be careful about giving advice, yet at times it is certainly appropriate to advise. "The teacher is ill-equipped to deal with the divorce issue in the most effective way," states Richard Gardner. "He or she has limited training to deal with such issues and is compromised even further by the fact that only partial information is being provided. Generally the information about the divorce comes from only one of the many parties involved" (in this case, the child).

Teachers are, however, in an ideal position to serve—really in a Band-Aid position. They can listen to the child who comes in to talk about the separation or divorce, can be a surrogate parent, or can serve as a good confidant. It is important to realize that they need not have all the answers. In fact, it's honest and appropriate to let children know that you don't have all the answers. To say, "Look I don't know what the answers are, but let's talk about it," is helpful to the child and is realistic.

CONFIDENTIALITY: The confidentiality issue is troublesome to teachers. "Should you betray a confidence?" they ask. Especially with teenagers, teachers are tempted to promise they'll keep whatever is being discussed confidential. But teachers should be careful about entering into an exclusive confidentiality relationship with a student of any age, for it puts the teacher in a position of great responsibility. The teacher who wants to help needs to know where to draw the line in the case of personal material that children disclose. The teacher must recognize his or her own limitations and know when to refer the child to a professional for counseling. Children should be referred in the following instances.

1. When a student expresses something dangerous to life and limb (about suicide or hurting himself or others), confidentiality must be broken. It is appropriate to give the child every chance to disclose information to a parent. It is appropriate to make every attempt to gain the child's approval for conveying the information to the proper professional. Indeed, children may tell a caring person because they want the information shared but can't share it themselves. "When the teacher tells the student he must inform someone else, there is the risk of the student's feeling traumatized because of the breach of confidentiality," states a child psychiatrist. "When the youngster shares something of this nature, however, part of him knows that it makes sense for a caring person to tell— even when it's against the child's will."

2. When a teacher is uncomfortable with the information the child is sharing, this is a cue that he cannot handle the information by himself and a professional needs to be contacted. At such times it makes sense for the teacher to say something to the child like, "This is very important information that you're telling me, and I'd like someone else to know about it too."

Teachers must remember how important it is to show respect for the child. Every attempt should be made either to give the child a chance to disclose important information or to gain the child's permission to share information. Yet the teacher must exercise his or her own best judgment about sharing the information and doesn't necessarily have to do it with the child's approval. In the case of informing a parent, *how* the confidence is shared is very important. Enlisting the aid of the school psychologist, social worker, or guidance counselor is strongly suggested at such times.

BECOMING OVERATTACHED: One of the risks of helping a youngster in crisis is becoming overattached to that youngster. When this happens, the teacher is likely to feel hurt, disappointed, or angry if the youngster is not appreciative of his or her efforts. The teacher also needs to remember that at certain times it is natural for a child to show negative feelings toward the teacher. It is, in fact, helpful to the child to be able to express these kinds of feelings. In addition, there will probably come a time when the child no longer wants to continue the relationship as such, and this may be hurtful to the teacher. Since the teacher's goal should be to offer support and to help the child to gain confidence in coping with and mastering difficult situations, the advice "Don't hold onto the child beyond what the child needs" should be heeded.

BECOMING OVERINVOLVED: Being overinvolved, as opposed to overattached, involves excessive empathy for the child, as opposed to a personal sense of hurt because the child is not appreciative. A warning of overinvolvement occurs when the teacher experiences "a strong gut feeling, rage, or identifying pain," according to one psychiatrist, who cautions, "Don't stop the relationship, but go slowly. Those feelings should be like yellow lights. Take inventory of what's triggering those feelings, then pay attention to how you're responding to the child." When a teacher becomes overinvolved, it is impossible to respond objectively, and objectivity is what the child needs.

TOUCHING: Young children (in kindergarten through third or fourth grade) may have a strong need to be cuddled or approvingly touched by teachers. The counselor in the specially funded program in Mill Valley reported that the children would climb all over a male teacher if he permitted it. For adolescent boys and girls who are experiencing emotional problems, however, being touched by a male teacher—even when the male teacher's intent is one of friendly concern or paternalism—may stir up uncomfortable feelings. Before touching an adolescent who's experiencing a crisis, the male teacher should be sensitive to how the student might interpret, for instance, a friendly hug or pat. On the other hand, there is no indication that distressed children of any age respond uncomfortably to being touched by a female teacher. This is probably because our society deems it acceptable for females to be demonstrative in a motherly manner. Although touching clearly does not have the same implications for all children, it may prove troublesome to some distressed adolescents.

One last thought on helping students: Emotions associated with a crisis do not just come to an end. As with most crises, there is a flurry of attention and activity while the separation or divorce is fresh, but after the flurry there comes the day-to-day experience of living with and coping with a new set of circumstances. The Reverend Gary Brown of the First Congregational Church, Stamford, Connecticut, believes in what he calls "structures for compassion." Although they were developed for people experiencing the death of a loved one, they seem equally applicable to youngsters experiencing separation and divorce. "The most compassionate kind of care is given through structures," he states. "You can pay attention to kids' needs when the parents are going through divorce and at crisis points, but if you do it strictly from compassion, in time you may move on to something else. There need to be ways of structuring compassion after the crisis period, to make sure you come back to the kid on a regular basis. I think that's important." These ways of "structuring" can be simple, regular activities such as noting on a calendar each week for the entire school year, "Check with Johnny."

Clearly, teachers are in a unique position to provide support to their students. Through the classroom environment they create and through the relationships they enter into, they can fulfill a variety of needs for students experiencing a crisis.

Teachers don't have to give affection or love. Everyone doesn't have the same capacity to care and needn't have. And teachers don't have to be psychologically oriented, trained, and skilled. But they can help their students to have a feeling of security and can help them to find a sense of direction. They can help them to develop a feeling of self-worth and to learn how to cope with and master difficult situations. Indeed, teachers can play a significant role. They can do more than they think they can.

7

Preventing Potential Problems

THERE are three reactions to parental separation
that may spill over into behavioral problems if not recognized and
attended to. The first is fear of abandonment. It is most commonly
seen in young children in the elementary grades. The second involves resolving loyalties to each parent, commonly called the loyalty conflict, which appears at all grade levels. It may surface at the
time of parental separation or remarriage, or at the time a child
reaches a new cognitive level. The third reaction involves a breakdown in coping ability that results in cutting classes or truancy.
This is most likely to occur at the secondary level. School professionals are in a position to deal with these reactions in a constructive and positive manner.

FEAR OF ABANDONMENT: A fear of being abandoned by their parents is common in youngsters between the ages of six and eleven. In
most cases children of this age group are still being nurtured and
are dependent on adults. So when one parent does actually move
out, it is easy to understand how some youngsters can develop a
real anxiety about being separated from the remaining parent. As
stated in chapter 4, these children may think that if their father
could leave them, their mother might also leave them, or that if
their mother could stop loving their father, she could stop loving
them too. The fear of abandonment may be so great that children
may resist leaving the custodial parent and may not want to go to
school, to lessons, or even to parties.

Fortunately, there is an effective way of helping children feel more secure when they are separated from a parent. All that is needed is a telephone and an adult who has the time and will make the effort to dial it. These children need to know where the parent is, that the parent is safe, when they will next see the parent, and where they will next see the parent. A telephone call can accomplish this.

One elementary school nurse tells about the child who arrived at school, came directly to her office, and asked to go home. "I feel very sad. I forgot my homework. I have to go home," the little girl announced. Since the nurse had been informed that the father had recently left, she suspected that the child needed to touch base with her mother. So the nurse phoned the mother, asked if someone could bring the homework to school, then said she thought Tammy would like to talk. When children come in feeling like this, the nurse often calls the parent and says, "Will you talk to Tammy for a moment? She needs to hear your voice." It is important for children to know the custodial parent's whereabouts in these instances. A telephone call can do a lot toward relieving the anxiety.

THE LOYALTY CONFLICT: Children, regardless of age, are suscep- tible to the pain and strain of the loyalty conflict. Sometimes it is exacerbated by parental actions. Sometimes it develops out of the child's own sensitivity regarding parental expectations. A twenty- nine-year-old married man whose parents recently divorced con- fided to his wife that he didn't know how he was going to allocate time fairly with each of his parents, for they were all going to be at the same party that weekend. If such a situation presents problems for an independent adult, what does it do to a dependent, school- age child?

The consequences for children who are deliberately or inadver- tently pulled in opposite directions by their parents can be very harmful. Teachers are justified in intervening and offering support to these youngsters in the following ways:
1. Help them to distinguish whether their sensitivity is causing the difficulty (as in the preceding example of the twenty-nine-

year-old and the example of the guilt-ridden teenager in example 1, below) or whether deliberate parental actions are responsible.

2. If parental actions are causing the conflict, let the children know that the problem really belongs to the parents, not to them, and help them to understand this. Let them know that it is legitimate to try to stay out of the middle, even though parents may try to involve them.

3. Offer these children some techniques for coping with the problem of divided loyalties.

The following examples illustrate problems created by the loyalty conflict and suggest ways to help resolve them.

Example 1: The high school sophomore described in chapter 4 confides, "I just can't say goodbye to them in the same room. I've got to say goodbye to my dad and goodbye to my mom in separate rooms. It's uncomfortable—I feel as though I'm doing something I shouldn't in front of the other—I mean kiss my mother goodbye and shake my father's hand."

The counselor, in this instance, first acknowledged how tough this must be and empathized with the teenager. She then tried to help him realize that it was his sensitivity to his parents that was causing him such conflict. Although he knew that his parents had great hostility toward each other, the counselor pointed out that they had made the decision to remain in the same house until the divorce was final, and they evidently chose to be in the same room at certain times. Therefore, they would most likely expect him to behave in the usual way when he was with them. If this was just too uncomfortable, the counselor suggested that the boy avoid speaking to them separately when they were together and instead give general responses intended for both of them. For example, he could poke his head in the door and say a general "Goodbye, I'm going to school—see you later."

Example 2: When Nancy visits her father each week, her father casually asks how Nancy's mother is, what she's doing, and if she has been going out. Nancy feels conflicted. Should she relay information about one parent to another? Is that disloyal? Will her father be angry if she doesn't answer? Will her mother be angry if she does?

It is legitimate to tell a youngster that he or she is not obliged to carry information about one parent to the other. If the divorced parents have questions about each other, they should ask and respond to each other, not use the child as a go-between. The child should be helped to realize that it is legitimate to stay out of the middle, and teachers can point out some responses that the child could use should the occasion arise. For example, "I don't feel good/comfortable/right talking to you about Mother/Father. Why don't you ask her/him?" or "I don't know" could be appropriate answers to questions children feel uncomfortable answering.

Example 3: Mrs. Robinson asks her sixteen-year-old daughter, Sara, to be home at two o'clock Sunday when her father is moving out. Sara is very upset by this prospect. She doesn't think she can stand being home to witness her father's departure. She doesn't want to hurt either parent.

This conflict was presented to Mr. Fein, a teacher who had been divorced. Mr. Fein pointed out that this was the mother's desire and the mother's problem. He made it clear to Sara that she had no obligation to be at home and suggested she tell her mother that it was too upsetting and that she wasn't planning to be home. Mr. Fein legitimized and supported Sara's right not to be home; Sara was most grateful. In addition, Sara was an honor student whose grades were slipping because of the stress surrounding the separation. Mr. Fein advised her, "Be selfish. If you don't feel like dealing with your family's problems, don't." Sara recalls that he implied, "Focus on your schoolwork; don't dwell on the other problems. It's insensitive of your parents to involve you, but you must provide your own way to escape thinking about the problems." "I always enjoyed studying," Sara confirms, "so I put myself into American history, which I loved. If I wasn't having a family life, I at least needed to have a school life."

Example 4: Fourteen-year-old Debbie, in the middle of her parents' custody battle, sadly reports: "Mother tried to turn me against my dad at every chance. If I dropped a dish, that would be because of the tension my dad was causing, according to her."

The guidance counselor explained to Debbie that her mother's anger at her father would very likely surface like this at other times. She also said that Debbie's father didn't need defending in these instances and that it was legitimate for her to remain silent when her mother made these accusations about her father. The counselor reiterated that this was a problem between the parents, that Debbie should try to stay out of the middle, and that refraining from comment at these times was the best strategy. Since Debbie was going through great, continual stress and pressure from both parents, the counselor provided her with continuous support. The counselor also received permission from Debbie to let each parent know that she was feeling "torn apart." In addition, possibilities for more formalized support from a psychologist or psychiatrist were discussed with Debbie and with each parent.

When the counselor spoke with each parent, she said something like, "You may not realize it—sometimes it's hard to see—but Debbie is feeling, as she puts it, "torn apart" because of conflicted loyalties. She wanted me to let you know this, and it certainly would be helpful to Debbie if you could be aware of her sensitivity and try to make things easier for her."

There are times when parents need to be made aware of the stress that they put on their children. Doing it with the child's permission is the ideal. Doing it without laying blame or guilt on the parent is a necessity.

CUTTING AND TRUANCY: Youngsters may feel so overwhelmed by the many adjustments they have to make during parental separation that they have great difficulty facing normal, everyday expectations. School, then, may become a great burden, for it signifies a place where discipline is required and where demands are made. Instead of confronting this burden, children may take what they perceive to be the easy way out. They may literally escape by cutting class or they may fail to go to school all together.

Either solution signals a deterioration in the youngsters' ability to cope and creates additional problems. Along with the self-knowledge that they're doing wrong, they are introducing further change in their lives by breaking the established routine of going to class. And routine is important in time of crisis. It's something to hold onto. School professionals, therefore, should move in quickly to terminate the truancy or cutting.

To do this effectively is, first of all, to be alert and to spot the problem before it becomes a habit. Next, these children should be confronted with the problem created by truancy or cutting. This should be done in a manner that conveys both firmness and understanding. Children should be given the option of deciding if, in fact, they need and want exceptions to be made *within the framework of the school structure*. Presenting options permits children to actively participate in determining their fate.

This active participation has the benefit of helping children move from a position of helplessness (in which everything is done to or for them) to a position of mastery. Perhaps it is legitimate to miss a class, to ask for an extension on an assignment, to miss a day of school. But the child is the one who will decide if these exceptions should be made, and when. School personnel can make this option available to truants and cutters, by saying something like, "I know that what you're going through can sometimes be difficult. Nevertheless, there are school rules. If there should be a time when you need a special favor let me know. I expect that you will not take advantage, but I also acknowledge that there may be times when missing class (having an assignment extended, etc.) would be very helpful."

The important fact to remember is that once a cutting or truancy pattern becomes established, it is very difficult to break. Not only have classes been missed, but accompanying assignments must be made up. It is often awkward to walk into a class after cutting it— the longer the class has been cut, the more difficult it is to reenter. And finally, cutters must work doubly hard to catch up at a time when their minds may not be functioning optimally, as their concentration may be on other, very important concerns. The teacher or administrator is in an ideal position to nip this potentially troublesome problem in the bud, and should do so. After all, school is the youngster's work. Work is routine. And routine is an important constant in times of crisis. During the period of parental separation and divorce, there are many unavoidable changes in the familiar routine. School should not be one of them.

8

Techniques for Handling Specific Problem Behavior

SEPARATION and divorce are crises. They dramatically punctuate a child's life. Yet they do not occur in a vacuum. Often the emotional climate leading to these events has been affecting the child's behavior well in advance of the event itself. Likewise, the events surrounding the later remarriage of a parent may result in temporary behavioral changes, even in children who seem to have adjusted well. In addition, the adjustment to divorce reoccurs every time a child reaches a new cognitive level or a new emotional plateau. So there is the potential for problem behavior all along the continuum.

While many children never exhibit problem behavior in the classroom, there are some common negative behavior patterns that children do exhibit. Verbal and physical bullying, attention seeking, stealing, crying, and fidgeting or restless behavior are readily observable. Equally prevalent, but less obvious, are daydreaming, fantasizing, regression, and somatic symptoms.

BULLYING: Bullying can result from the child's need to express anger in an aggressive way, or from the need to enhance self-esteem or maintain self-image (especially if things are happening at home that make the child feel put down). Bullying can also result from a sense of helplessness and frustration that comes from being in an uncontrollable situation. In this latter case, the child feels that if he can at least control something, there is hope that he can eventually control—in this instance—his family situation.

Six-year-old Billy was the biggest bully who ever lived, according to his recently remarried mother. At recess, for example, when the youngsters were playing a game and things didn't go his way, he would first yell at his classmates in an intimidating way. If this didn't get the results he wanted, he grabbed them and hit them. He tried to bully not only his classmates but the teacher as well. For instance, on one occasion when the class was lining up to take a trip, Billy pushed his way into the line. When the teacher pointed this out, Billy yelled at the teacher that he was in his rightful place and he wasn't going to move.

How should the teacher handle bullying? *Don't allow it.* Instead of bending over backward to be sympathetic, quickly stop the bullying. Although the youngster may initially feel better if he takes a punch at a classmate, this kind of behavior will get him in trouble in the long run. Not only will he lose friends and possibly be physically hurt in one of the encounters, but if allowed to get away with it, he will probably gain the reputation of being a bully; and it is difficult to undo a reputation. In addition, the psychological factors that triggered the initial bullying will be compounded by yet another emotion: *guilt;* for the bully knows he's doing wrong.

In Billy's case, he had a teacher whom his mother described as "old-fashioned and a strict disciplinarian, but loving." This teacher wouldn't let Billy get away with anything. Furthermore, she encouraged the other boys in the class not to stand for the bullying. She was sensitive to the reasons children bully, and whenever possible, after one of his aggressive encounters, she would take Billy aside and say something like, "I know you aren't angry at Johnny. Can you tell me what's the matter?" and she would encourage Billy to talk. She also told him that he could stand outside the classroom whenever he felt angry, and that when he felt under control he could come back. In the beginning she had to send him out of class when he got angry, but as the year progressed, he would walk out by himself when he felt his anger rising. "To have a friend, you have to be a friend," the teacher impressed upon Billy. And Billy wanted friends, so rather than take out his anger on a classmate, Billy would often (though not always) make use of his option to leave the room.

A very different experience was recalled by Mrs. Bergstrom, a single parent. Her son's sixth-grade teacher was nice and sympathetic, but not a strong disciplinarian. "One kid got away with murder—called the teacher a bastard in front of the class, along with other verbal abuse. This kid's parents were divorcing, so it made the other kids aware of his problems in a very negative way. I guess the teacher was trying to be understanding, but he ended up losing the respect of his students, and he made it worse for the kid with the problem. Kids that are in crisis need limits like everyone else. Allowing glaring exceptions doesn't help anyone, especially the child," Mrs. Bergstrom observed.

Even when the teacher can put an end to bullying, the underlying need to be aggressive is not necessarily satisfied. "Bullies must have their chance at being boss in other things," concluded a second-grade teacher. "Usually they need to be built up, and I build them up in other ways. For example, I have a classmate of the week—a whole bulletin board is devoted to the student and his or her artifacts. Or I try to find a way to make the bully important, like letting him be a line leader; or I give him a special responsibility, like being in charge of the hamster."

Opinions vary as to whether or not teachers should encourage physical activities that legitimize angry, aggressive behavior. These activities could provide an acceptable outlet for the youngster who needs to take out his anger in a physical way. A punching bag, for example, could well be a worthwhile investment for use in the elementary classroom. Yet some professionals disagree, reasoning that hitting a punching bag does not enable the youngster to understand the cause of his anger and therefore only relieves the immediate problem. Nevertheless, punching bags, soft balls (like sponge balls), and pillows can effectively relieve immediate aggressive needs, while admittedly not providing long-range psychological benefits.

Bullying signifies a problem. The teacher should move in quickly to stop it and should not make allowances. The teacher can, however, provide opportunities for the bully to enhance his self-esteem in acceptable ways. The teacher can provide opportunities for him to talk about what's bothering him and can help him to differentiate between angry thoughts and feelings and angry behavior. The teacher is in a position to provide support and understanding to the child who bullies. If the bullying continues, however, additional help through the school psychologist is indicated.

ATTENTION SEEKING: The behavior of the smart aleck or the class clown, like that of the bully, can hardly be ignored by either teacher or student. These children work hard to get attention, possibly because their parents are too wrapped up in their own problems to pay them sufficient attention at home. In dealing with these youngsters, the same philosophy that is used with the bully applies. The behavior should immediately be stopped so that these children don't acquire a reputation that must then be maintained.

Teachers should be very careful, however, not to "put down" attention-seeking youngsters, even when a put-down would surely put an end to the disruptive classroom behavior. Attention seeking signifies a need for recognition. Egos need building, not deflating. Providing acceptable ways for these youngsters to gain recognition, while curbing the acting-out behavior, is the goal.

One seventeen-year-old boy, admitting he'd been "a wise guy until a year ago," observed that often teachers can successfully intimidate attention-seeking youngsters so that they don't act out in class. Intimidation clearly does not resolve the emotional need that initially triggered the attention seeking. Intimidation may, in fact, compound these youngsters' problems, for it may trigger anger at the teacher who has successfully stifled their bids for attention.

Teachers can, however, be effective with many "wise guys" if they can establish a personal relationship with these students outside of the normal class time. During this extra time, teachers should try to convey a sense of respect and recognition of worth to the youngster, while acknowledging the problem that attention-seeking behavior creates in the classroom. Through this interaction, the youngster learns that the teacher cares enough to try to understand the reasons for the acting-out behavior and is given the chance to talk. The youngster is thus receiving positive adult recognition. And adult attention may be especially important if it is lacking at home.

When dealing with attention-seeking students, then, teachers should make themselves available and look for legitimate (not contrived) ways to let these children know that they're worthwhile. Through both personal and classroom experiences, attention seekers can be given acceptable outlets.

Another behavior that may appear to be attention seeking is a seemingly endless need to talk about the family situation. While the teacher and classmates may not want to hear any more from the child, this kind of talk is beneficial. For each time the child discusses the subject, although pain may be clearly evident, there is a desensitization process operating. In other words, each time the child talks about the separation, it becomes more bearable.

Elementary school teachers have many opportunities for allowing these kinds of feelings to be shared. Magic circles, show and tell, and rap sessions encourage verbal sharing. Thought books, "me books," diaries, and private journals facilitate this sharing in writing. One high school teacher commented, "Everything that happens is grist for an English teacher's mill. It's always amazing how kids open up and tell about their intimate lives."

Indeed, this observation was confirmed by a sixteen-year-old boy, who had spoken to no adults about his parents' divorce. "I was reading *How Green Was My Valley* for English. We were supposed to do a paper about how depression had affected our family. I wrote about the divorce." For Tom, a high school senior, the essay on the college application provided an opportunity to reveal his feelings and concerns (see p. 66). Writing to an unknown audience allowed him to reflect upon his present situation (and perhaps shape his future).

STEALING: Parents in the midst of separation and divorce understandably become preoccupied with their feelings and problems. As a consequence, the love and affection that they once routinely bestowed on their children may be in short supply (or even temporarily nonexistent). One way that children (usually below the fifth grade) deal with this loss is to steal—mostly meaningless items—in an effort to make up for the lost love and security. Children may also steal as a way of calling attention to themselves and as a way of punishing their parents for not loving them. Or children may steal because they feel that they need to be punished for some (often unconscious) guilt feelings that they harbor.

These young stealers must be dealt with when caught. That is reality. It is wrong to take something that doesn't belong to them, and this must be impressed upon them. In some cases they should return the stolen object to its owner with an apology. But this should not be forced upon children who may be hurting too much to go through the humiliation of an apology. In any event, returning the object and apologizing does not get to the underlying problem, and this is where a skillful teacher or the school counselor, social worker, or psychologist can be helpful. The fact that the teacher, counselor, social worker, or psychologist knows that the child didn't need the stolen item should be communicated understandingly to the child. And the child should be encouraged to talk. If the child can express his feelings to someone, this may be the beginning of the end, as far as the stealing episodes are concerned. Nevertheless, the previous caution of making referrals when the information a youngster shares is discomforting to a teacher applies. The fact that an understanding and sensitive teacher can unlock the emotional gate that allows a youngster to talk is highly valued. But a person with advanced training in psychology is probably the best resource to ultimately help children who continue to steal. These children will usually need professional help in working through and in resolving their problems.

CRYING: The pervasive sadness that children feel when their parents separate was discussed in chapter 4. Crying is one manifestation of this sadness and is a common reaction to which teachers must respond. The following experience, recalled by a seventeen-year-old girl, is a good illustration of the problem and of appropriate responses on the part of school personnel.

When my parents split up I was eleven and start-
ing junior high school. I don't really remember the
bad things that went on, like the fighting, because
my mind wants to forget all that. I do remember
crying a lot and the helpful people who alleviated
the pain. When I entered my first day of junior
high my father left. I was very upset and cried most
of the day. I don't know how my teacher found
out about my parents' separation, but she was very
sensitive to my situation. She asked me privately,
in the hall, why I was crying. She did not embarrass me in front of the entire class. Then she suggested that I see my counselor. I wasn't sure at the
time whether it would help me, but in retrospect, it
was one of the major contributions in helping me
adjust to my new situation. I cried a lot during my
sessions and my counselor said to let it out, that
that helps. She asked me, if I could have one wish,
what would it be? I said, "To get my parents back
together." She had said that she would call my
parents and talk to them only if I wanted her to. I
agreed to it because I wanted to be helped and
have my pain alleviated.

Crying for me at the time of the separation was
helpful. I didn't cry to get attention as some children of separated parents do. I cried because I was
really hurting inside.

If children do cry in classes or in school, the teacher should respond
in a supportive manner that will not embarrass the student, as this
teenager suggests.

RESTLESSNESS: When the stability in children's lives has been
shaken, restlessness and fidgety behavior may result. Incessant
drumming on desks, the need to be continually in and out of seats,
the repeated sharpening of pencils, throwing of things in wastebas-

kets, opening and closing of window blinds—these actions cause distractions to teachers and students. Since these are reactions to shaken stability, teachers need to be consistent in their behavior and expectations, even though these children are suffering inside. Teachers can thus provide some needed stability, at least in the classroom. As stated in chapter 3, consistency should not be confused with rigidity. Caring and understanding are clearly indicated and should be communicated. But these youngsters must also be made aware that certain expectations apply to everyone in the classroom. Setting limits in these instances supplies some degree of structure. Structure provides some degree of stability. Consistency on the part of the teacher makes this all possible.

Although the kinds of behavior previously described are readily observable and usually require specific and direct intervention, there are equally important kinds of behavior that are less obvious, less disruptive, and less responsive to direct intervention on the part of the teacher. Fantasizing, daydreaming, regression, and somatic symptoms are such behaviors. They serve a useful purpose for people in crisis by protecting them from having to confront an emotionally painful reality before they're emotionally ready to handle it.

DAYDREAMING: Daydreaming is a solitary pastime. It provides a safe haven where the mind can wander to escape psychological distress. For children coping with parental separation, daydreaming can provide temporary relief from a myriad of unpleasant, anxiety-producing thoughts.

One elementary school psychologist relates that teachers will come to her office and discuss their concerns about daydreaming: "I don't know what's going on. Johnny just doesn't seem to be with the class—he's somewhere else." This psychologist lets teachers know that it is OK for a child to daydream, especially in the weeks immediately following psychological trauma. Daydreaming contributes to the desensitizing process that must take place before acceptance of the new situation can occur. As the child adjusts to the new situation, however, the daydreaming should decrease. Thus, teachers need to be concerned with the duration and intensity—not the occurrence—of daydreaming.

FANTASIZING: Another contributor to the desensitizing process is fantasizing. It is not necessarily a solitary occupation, however, since fantasies can be shared with others. There is a definite value in sharing fantasies, and teachers should be aware of this fact. Fantasy enables a person to think about a distressing situation that may otherwise be unthinkable. And sharing a fantasy can be a form of problem solving: in the process of verbalizing the fantasy, one begins to come to terms with it. Thus, when teachers provide opportunities for the sharing of fantasies, they may at the same time be allowing students in crisis to make progress in coming to terms with their situation. In addition, fears and insecurities may be revealed through fantasy, and indeed, some fantasies may be frightening to the child. So alert teachers should seek additional professional help for the student if appropriate. As stated previously, when teachers feel uncomfortable with the material the child is divulging, additional professional help is clearly indicated.

A common fantasy verbalized by children is that of having their separated parents reunited. Judith Wallerstein reports that this fantasy continued to persist ten years after the divorce in half of the children who had been preschoolers when the Children of Divorce Project began. She further reports that "Whether absent or visiting regularly or erratically . . . the noncustodial father remained a significant psychological presence in the lives of his children. . . . A heightened need to establish relationships with absent fathers appeared to occur as these youngsters, especially the girls, reached adolescence."[1] Often, well-meaning, sympathetic adults will try to offer reassurance and hope to these youngsters, but this is inappropriate. As the poignant exchange

1. Judith S. Wallerstein, "Children of Divorce: Preliminary Report of a 10-Year Follow-up of Young Children," *American Journal of Orthopsychiatry* 54, no. 3 (July 1984) pp. 451–54, 457.

between Hopeful and Ann Landers illustrates, this kind of response is not helpful to the child, although it may make the adult feel better. What is helpful is the fact that a caring adult is listening and allowing the child to verbalize and to thereby make progress toward coping with the situation. The adult who creates opportunites for a child to share fantasies, who takes the time—or makes the time—to listen to these fantasies, is performing an invaluable service. And the adult most likely to be initially effective in this endeavor is the school professional—the classroom teacher, the school counselor, or the school psychologist.

Dear Ann:
My parents were divorced when I was ten. I'll be 16 soon and have not seen my father for four years, although he has visiting rights. I think about him a lot.

Just before Christmas I asked my teacher if I should write him a letter telling him about my interests. She said, "Yes, but don't let your mother know."

I wrote a long letter and sent a small picture of myself. I haven't received an answer. Should I write again and ask if my letter got lost in the Christmas rush?—Hopeful

Dear H.:
Your teacher gave you bad advice. If you know where your dad is, he knows where YOU are. Let him be.

It's not hard to build fantasies around a daddy who isn't there. Don't let your imagination trick you into thinking he is something he is not, honey.

April 29, 1977
Ann Landers

REGRESSION: When other ways of coping fail, regression may develop. Children experiencing a crisis that they cannot deal with may well feel powerless and helpless. Their security threatened, these children may regress to an earlier behavioral stage where they remember life as being less difficult and more secure. As described in chapter 4, clinging, whining, and looking for laps to sit on are common characteristics in primary-grade youngsters. Increased dependence on the teacher is common in older children. In general, these children may revert to what the teacher sees as immature behavior. When it is understood that the immature behavior is an attempt to act younger because the child simply can't contend with the emotional burden, the distinction between intentionally bothersome behavior and regressive behavior becomes clear.

Dealing with the intentionally bothersome act would be different, then, from dealing with the bothersome act triggered by regression. The latter act is not an act of naughtiness. Although the teacher may not realize this the first time a youngster engages in bothersome behavior and may, in fact, admonish or scold, one who is alert will realize that this is unusual behavior for the child after it occurs a second or third time. At this point, rather than respond with something like, "Cut it out! Big boys/girls don't whine/cry/cling," or "High school students don't . . ." the teacher might well say something like, "You're not acting like yourself today," and might follow up that sentence with, "Is something upsetting you?" or "Is something on your mind?" By acknowledging that the child isn't his or her normal self, the teacher is conveying understanding and at the same time offering the child a chance to talk.

Regression is an adaptive behavior and should be short-lived if the emotional climate is supportive enough. It is therefore valid for children in crisis to be allowed a limited period of time for regressive behavior. If the regression becomes more than a temporary phenomenon or if the teacher feels concerned, the school counselor and psychologist should be consulted and the parent(s) alerted.

SOMATIC SYMPTOMS: Physical symptoms that are unconsciously, psychologically generated are difficult to distinguish from aches and pains with other causes. Thus, they should be treated and responded to, not ignored or devalued.

The child who always asks to go to the bathroom, the student who continually wants to go to the nurse—these youngsters may indeed cause teachers frustration. Nevertheless, accusing these youngsters of feigning illness is not productive since somatic symptoms are not an attempt to pretend illness but entail actual pain.

Nurse Nellie of the Meadow Elementary School fondly recalls Lizzy. Lizzy's dad left the family toward the end of her second-grade school year. Before his departure, she began having pains. Lizzy's mother phoned the school nurse to inform her of this and indicated that the pains could be psychosomatic. Nevertheless, she wanted the nurse to be aware of Lizzy, to support her, and to send her back to class if appropriate. "When they come in with any pain or hurt, it gets treated," explains Nurse Nellie. "We use ice on hurting muscles, no matter what. They lie down and I ask, 'Are you getting sick or is something bothering you?' There's a different body quality that goes with physical and emotional pain. In Lizzy's case, quietness let you know it was sadness." Nurse Nellie administered an ice pack to Lizzy's hurt each time she came in; she'd stay for about ten minutes, and then she'd return to class.

When schools are fortunate enough to have a nurse like Nellie, classroom teachers can send children like Lizzy to the nurse and know that they are not imposing. Teachers do not have to be concerned with diagnosis, and the child receives some extra attention and nurturing, which may be needed to help the child reach acceptance and go on to the next emotional step.

When schools do not have a full-time nurse, the psychologist, social worker, guidance counselor, or principal can provide support. Perhaps a quiet corner of the classroom—if there is a designated area where children may go to play quiet games, watch the frog or hamster, or read books, but not talk—is secluded enough to relieve the child of the stress that is producing the ache or pain. This latter suggestion is appropriate only when no other support persons are available, however.

Adolescents experience somatic symptoms, of course, but responding to them often seems more complicated, for adolescents are more prone to manipulation and may feign illness as an excuse to avoid responsibility. One high school counselor relates that teachers come to her office and understandably express anger when they feel students are trying to take advantage. If the teacher has been excusing the student repeatedly, the teacher wants assurance that it is legitimate. If the teacher hasn't allowed the student to leave, there is a guilty feeling—perhaps the request *was* legitimate. Since teenagers readily admit that they may use the divorce as an excuse for not doing what's expected, and since they also say that setting limits is helpful and is a way of showing caring, this counselor suggests that teachers tell the student of their concern without making a judgment. This can be accomplished by using observation, as the following example illustrates. Teacher: "Susie, I'm concerned. I notice you've asked to leave class a lot lately, and you've missed some important discussions and one quiz. Is there something I should know about? Can I help in any way?"

After hearing the student's response, in most cases teachers should work with the student in setting up a realistic schedule to make up the missed work. Students easily misperceive the quantity of work entailed in catching up as well as the amount of time it takes to do an adequate job. To put in the time and not achieve the desired results would be a negative experience these youngsters can't afford to have. It is legitimate, then, for teachers to take the initiative as long as the students are actively involved. The goal is to make up the missed work. Once this is achieved, students should feel a sense of accomplishment and a sense of mastery. And these feelings of success should provide the climate for the youngsters' emotional growth to continue in a healthier way.

It should be clear from the preceding examples that specific techniques and strategies do make a difference when dealing with problem behavior in the classroom. Since there is the possibility that this behavior may be triggered by a serious emotional problem, and since teachers are often the first ones to notice behavioral changes, it is advisable to inform the parent(s) of observable behavior changes. In these instances, the good judgment and the alertness of the teacher are invaluable. As one Scarsdale psychiatrist stated, "Children come to me after a problem has been spotted, and often it is the classroom teacher who brings attention to the problem in the first place."

TOM'S COLLEGE APPLICATION ESSAY

I come from a home that is almost broken. That is, my parents are in the process of getting divorced. I guess that everyone thinks that their situation is unique and devastating; I do not know if mine really is, but the whole ordeal has been pretty unbearable for me. My parents announced their decision to separate in July. They have both continued to live in the house to date. I was not shocked when my parents announced that they were going to get a divorce. I know this statement may sound callous and insensitive, but divorce had been threatened before many times by both sides and was not a new issue. When they officially announced that they were getting divorced, I was surprised how upset I was. Even though I had always rationally expected them to divorce someday, the fait accompli was hard for me to handle. Even now, while writing this, I have mixed feelings. I really do not wish that they would stay married, but at the same time, the idea of divorce is a little frightening to me.

This past year the tension in the house has been unbearable. My parents have grown to hate and despise each other more and more, all in front of my eyes. It is not possible for me to describe how torn I feel when I see them not even arguing, but viciously attacking each other. When I witness one of these scenes, I often visualize a perfect home where my father would come home every day at 5:15 and mother would run out and give him a kiss.

While daydreaming, I sometimes wish they would unite against me. This statement sounds really weird, but the constant war for my affections is utterly draining. My parents invariably disagree with each other on everything. Thus, I just take the opinion that suits my purposes. It would be nice to have them be a unified force. I know this sounds corny, but I think I miss the security of having two parents to rely on together.

In all, I guess I have such mixed feelings about their divorce because I am afraid of how it will change my life. This fear sounds a little selfish, but it is very real. This January my parents are going to court and will finally become divorced. On this application I had trouble deciding if I should check the divorced box. When the application asks who has custody, I am dumbfounded because I do not know who will have custody come January. I do not know whether or not to file a financial aid application because who will pay for my college is not yet settled. These problems may sound insignificant, and individually they are; but taken as a whole they become oppressive. I feel like part of my future is on hold until January.

Do not misunderstand me, my life has not been a living hell. Last year was my best academic year ever. I do appreciate the freedom and responsibility I am given. And I guess because my parents do not communicate with each other at all, I have become their confidant. Because of their loss of each other, I have in some respects risen to the position of an equal. I have a lot more responsibility than most of my peers when it comes to family decisions. In total, I think I have gained a lot of adult experiences that an ordinary 17-year-old would never have had. But I feel that I really missed out on something by not coming from an intact home.

9

The Use of School Resources

PSYCHIATRISTS, psychologists, social workers, guidance counselors, school nurses, and teachers are generally acknowledged as the support people for youngsters in crisis. Yet there are five additional resources within most school systems. School secretaries, male paraprofessionals and older male students, librarians, and extracurricular activities are potential sources of support, role models, information, and a sense of belonging.

SCHOOL SECRETARIES: When parents contact the school, often the first person they encounter is a secretary. Secretaries, in fact, may become aware of family problems before the principal, teachers, and professional support staff. Secretaries are rarely provided with specific training to equip them to deal, in person or over the telephone, with people in crisis. They respond intuitively. Yet this initial response may set the tone for the parents' feelings about sharing information with the school.

Parents say that they appreciate secretaries who handle confidential information in a businesslike way. This enables the parents to impart emotionally charged information more easily. To say, "We appreciate your giving us this information," or to offer a waiting parent a cup of coffee or a magazine is not inappropriate and may ease the strain on parents. Responses such as "Oh, how sad," "That's too bad," "Oh dear!," and even "I'm sorry" are not appropriate responses to parents coming in to discuss separation and divorce. These responses, on the other hand, might well be appropriate when parents impart information about death, accident, and serious illness.

Some parents, given a willing listener, will routinely tell secretaries about all of their problems. This takes time from the secretary's designated responsibilities. As long as the secretary makes no judgments and offers no advice, however, "lending an ear" may be helpful to parents—if the secretary has the time to spare.

Children gravitate toward understanding, caring, nurturing people. Often they seem to seek out a particular secretary to share conversation, if not problems. After all, secretaries are more available than teachers and designated support people and can offer nurturing and understanding. One principal's secretary almost always puts a basket of candy on her desk and often makes change for students who need telephone money. She continually has a small, dedicated group of emotionally needy youngsters in the office because it's a place that feels good—it's another refuge.

Because of the impact that secretaries have, it seems appropriate for school administrators to develop a simple presentation aimed at sensitizing secretaries to ways of handling people in crisis more effectively. (For example, a sensitive secretary could certainly help the school nurse phone parents, as described in chapter 7.) Unquestionably, secretaries are in a position to perform a distinct and valuable service to people in crisis, and their capabilities should be tapped.

MALE PARAPROFESSIONALS AND HIGH SCHOOL STUDENTS: Chapter 3 discusses the importance of male role models in the development of children living with their mothers. Paul C. Glick, senior demographer in the Population Division of the Census Bureau in 1979, reported that the *proportion* of children under eighteen living with their mothers only *at a given point in time* is expected to go from 8 percent in 1960 to 23 percent in 1990.[1] (It rose to 20 percent in 1982.) A breakdown of the proportion of children under eighteen

1. "Children of Divorced Parents in Demographic Perspective," *Journal of Social Issues* 35, no. 4 (1979): 176.

living with their mothers only in 1982 was reported in a Census Bureau publication as follows:[2]

White: 15.3%

Black: 47.2%

Spanish origin (per Census Bureau may be of any race): 25.3%

One can infer from these statistics that (1) a significant and growing number of children could benefit from the availability of good male role models, and (2) there is a particular need for males of black and Spanish origin. As previously stated, only a small percentage (16.9 percent) of elementary school teachers are male. And an even smaller percentage of *that* small percentage come from minority groups. Where, then, does one find males who can serve as good role models?

The answer lies in the hiring of more male paraprofessionals and in the recruiting of male high school students to voluntarily assist in elementary schools. The former are already employed in schools, often as security guards. Is it possible to hire young men enrolled in community college programs to assist part-time, for example, in the math labs, reading labs, classrooms? Clearly a concerted effort to add male paraprofessionals to the elementary school staff is in order.

Local high school boys, who would be good role models, should be actively sought to volunteer in elementary schools. These boys obviously have neither the time nor the training to work as regularly as paraprofessionals. But they can assist teachers in the classroom and can help on the playground without a large time commitment. And they needn't be top students. There has, in fact, been success using underachievers in this capacity.

The feeling of personal success that high school students gain from volunteering in an elementary school classroom is easy to understand. Young children look at teenage boys with awe and often treat them as heroes. One learning-disabled senior—a football player, but certainly not the star—assisted a third-grade teacher twice a week. On the days he was scheduled to come, the

2. U.S. Bureau of the Census, Current Population Reports, Series P-20, no. 380, *Marital Status and Living Arrangements*, March 1982, p. 5.

children eagerly awaited his arrival and would cling to him and hug him as he entered the room. Imagine his delight when a pint-sized rooting section showed up at the football game one weekend! He was a hero to these youngsters. And they, in turn, contributed to his feelings of worth.

Volunteer work can certainly be done without training, but students working with young children should be given a brief overview of the characteristics of the particular age group involved, and they should be made aware of teacher expectations before beginning their work. A fourth-grade teacher in the Bronx, New York, whose class is one-third black, one-third Hispanic, and one-third white, relates that her principal asked if she would like a high school volunteer. Her initial enthusiasm turned to dismay when a teenager in a provocative outfit arrived, causing further distraction to a class whose attention span was already very short. The teenager had no idea what was expected of her, and the teacher, with a class of thirty-five youngsters who needed constant supervision, had no time to adequately instruct the young woman. It was an unhappy experience for all concerned.

Happier results have been achieved by juniors and seniors at suburban Scarsdale High School in New York who volunteer at five local elementary schools in conjunction with a Human Development course that they select as an elective. In this way, students learn about human development in theory and also gain practical experience at the elementary school near their home.

Establishing a volunteer program between elementary schools and the local high school takes organization and cooperation between the adult liaisons in each school. Girls seem to gravitate toward this kind of program. The challenge, then, is to make this program initially attractive to older boys with whom youngsters can identify and respect. The initial investment of time to properly organize and select students should be worth the final outcome: a steady supply of good male role models for youngsters of elementary school age.

SCHOOL LIBRARIANS: The school library is well known as an information-giving resource. It is the school librarian, however, who can generate interest in specific materials that the library has to offer. The librarian is thus in a key position to acquaint staff, students, and parents with the availability of literature on divorce.

Theme-oriented book lists, compiled by the librarian, can provide a ready reference. For example, a list of books under the title "Divorce Literature," with grade-level designations where appropriate, is helpful to staff members for use in the classroom and for making reading suggestions to students and their parents. At the secondary level, these lists can be posted in the library; they can also be reproduced and made available for students' personal use. One librarian writes a regular column in her elementary school's newsletter. After a brief introduction, she presents reading lists that can be clipped and saved for future reference. Sometimes her introduction is on "Recent Acquisitions," followed by a list; at other times she focuses on a specific subject, such as "Divorce Books" or the broader topic "Crisis Books."

There are many ways of generating interest in books. For example, librarians may set up book displays. Although some librarians say that they don't feel comfortable devoting an entire display to books on divorce, these books could be included in a display featuring life changes (birth, death, illness, moving, etc.). Many librarians present special library talks to classes. Including life-changes or crisis books in the discussion would certainly be appropriate. There are librarians who express discomfort with the whole idea of introducing sweet, innocent children to the harsh realities of life before they actually must face them. One elementary school librarian who expresses this viewpoint is nevertheless the first one to be of help when a crisis occurs. She has provided many parents with appropriate literature for themselves and their youngsters. And she has taped the most popular of the divorce books for young readers. That way they can listen to the tape while reading or looking at the book. "It makes it a lot easier for them," she noted.

Should children be protected from the harsh realities of life until they must actually face them? "Children should be exposed to all crisis situations *before*," advocates Ann Kliman, director of the Situational Crisis Service at the Center for Preventive Psychiatry in

White Plains, New York, and author of *Crisis: Psychological First Aid for Recovery and Growth.* "If we pretend they don't know and don't understand, it may feel more comfortable to us, but children should·be given the chance to master an event before it affects them. . . . When things are far enough away not to overwhelm, then is the time to introduce them so children can learn to understand and cope with them."

Teachers and librarians who feel comfortable introducing children to feelings and problems through books should find the following books (annotated in the Bibliography) helpful: *Books to Help Children Cope with Separation and Loss* (appropriate for three- to sixteen-year-olds), *Helping Children Cope: Mastering Stress through Books and Stories* (for children four to eight), *Helping Children Cope with Separation and Loss* (for elementary school youngsters), and *The Bookfinder* (for children two to fifteen).

It must be remembered that people going through separation or divorce don't necessarily think of reading to ease their burden. Yet there are many appropriate and useful books in print. The librarian is in a position to make these resources known and should be encouraged to do so.

EXTRACURRICULAR ACTIVITIES: Participation in an activity and membership in a group produce a sense of belonging. If youngsters can find a sense of community in an activity, it can hold them together while other aspects of their life may be falling apart. Further, being an integral part of a group effort generates a feeling of self-worth and accomplishment.

During the period of parental separation, youngsters should be encouraged to pursue an interest in a formalized way—whether in music, art, drama, sports, youth groups, or interest-centered clubs (French club, chess club, etc.). "What works about extracurricular activities is that kids are taking the first steps out of their family and need a temporary tribe to try out behavior and thoughts. If a kid has this kind of group, it makes a big difference," observes the adviser of a church youth group.

Participation in activities may provide an escape. At such times youngsters will no doubt direct a disproportionate amount of energy toward the activity, and other worthwhile endeavors, such as schoolwork, may take a back seat. Over the short run, the value to be gained from such participation probably outweighs the lack of attention to routine demands. Nevertheless, youngsters should be encouraged to be responsible in meeting the important demands. And this is where the adult in charge can be helpful.

Adults who are coaches, leaders, or advisers for activities need to be aware of the special value that these activities *and the adult in charge* have for youngsters in crisis. Often the supervising adult becomes a role model for these youngsters; sometimes the adult becomes a friend who can offer guidance and support.

In all cases (except where youngsters turn to youth gang participation), involvement in extracurricular activities should provide a positive support system for youngsters whose parents have separated.

In a school system, the potential resources for helping students in crisis are many. Recognizing them and activating them is the challenge. Seeing them successfully help needy students is the reward.

10

The Noncustodial Parent: Requests and Rights

Letter from a noncustodial father

29 August 1983

Superintendent of Schools
Scarsdale Board of Education
Scarsdale, N.Y. 10583

Dear Sir:

In the divorce decree of March 1983, it was declared that I as the father would receive copies of the children's report cards from my ex-wife. To date I've received none (although after repeated phone calls, she claims to have sent them and will send duplicates).

Owing to the fact that my ex-wife has not spoken to me in about two years (which may help to explain the nonexistent report cards) and I have no ax to grind, except in the best interests of my kids, I'd appreciate your help in obtaining same.

I'd do *anything* in order to help the situation, even having them mailed to court as an intermediary.

Very truly yours,

NONCUSTODIAL parents span the spectrum, from those who are highly involved and interested to those who have abandoned their children physically and emotionally. Regardless of involvement, two factors deserve attention. First, within the post-divorce family the child's relationship with the noncustodial parent continues to be of significant importance. Second, schools are inexperienced in dealing with noncustodial parents, yet they have the obligation, when requested, to inform the noncustodial parent of the child's school progress, unless there's a court order prohibiting release of this information.

The Children of Divorce Project data indicate that the child's relationship with the noncustodial father affects the child's self-esteem. Low self-esteem and depression were linked to infrequent visits by the noncustodial father; high self-esteem and ego functioning were related to frequent visits. Since fathers comprise 90 percent of noncustodial parents, it would appear that every effort should be made to involve most noncustodial fathers in their children's lives. While this is an easy recommendation to make, it is more difficult to accomplish.

It takes a concerted effort on the part of the noncustodial parent (who will hereafter be referred to in the masculine gender) to have a relationship with his children. Usually this is accomplished through visits, or "visitations," to use the legal term. While these visits may indeed be important for children, they often entail delicate orchestration on the part of the adults involved.

Visitations are not a natural happening. They are a creation of the courts. The when and where of visitations are spelled out in the divorce decree, which often includes the most specific details (such as whether the father can enter the house when he comes to pick up the children). For noncustodial fathers who have regular contact with their children by telephone, visitations become part of an ongoing relationship. For others, visitations occur in a vacuum and may, at best, be awkward.

Interestingly, the Children of Divorce Project data showed that the quality of the preseparation father-child relationship does not have a direct bearing on the frequency of the father's visitations. Indeed, the father who seemed uninterested before the divorce may realize how easily he can lose all relationship with his children and may become surprisingly attentive. On the other hand, the father who is very close to his children may find it painful to see them under these new circumstances. The simple act of returning to the home where he and his children shared happy experiences, for example, may prove emotionally difficult. In addition, fathers who are depressed and fathers who feel guilty—regardless of the preseparation relationship—find it difficult to maintain close ties with their children.

Distance also becomes a factor. Custodial mothers may remarry and move, or they may relocate to take advantage of new opportunities. This presents additional challenges to an ongoing relationship, as the following experiences illustrate.

"They went to Massachusetts," relates a noncustodial father, now remarried. "It was devastating to me. The boys came down for a visit every third weekend, but this prevented them from participating in sports. So I finally said they didn't have to come regularly. You know, I have a son who plays football. He's good. I've never seen him play. . . . The distance is hard. . . . My kids. I still cry when they leave—each time."

"I've given up and abandoned the children," admits another noncustodial father, whose ex-wife remarried and immediately took the children two thousand miles away. "I didn't know where they were. A year and a half later, the kids were in trouble and I went out to see them. When I contacted the school, I was treated like a nonperson. It was futile. It seems to me the school's having its hands full with two lousy kids and should have been glad to discover a father who may have helped. I went to the principal's office and asked to be put on a mailing list. I was told, 'Fine.' Yet I never received a thing."

A variety of circumstances, then, influence visitations. Indeed, a noncustodial father's interest in his children cannot be accurately judged by the frequency of visitations. Nevertheless, the relationship between a noncustodial parent and his children remains of great importance. With these facts in mind, parents and school professionals need to address the following questions:

1. What is the role of the school vis-à-vis the noncustodial parent?
2. What could it be?
3. What should it be?

At present, schools do very little to involve the noncustodial parent in his child's education. Often, in fact, school professionals ignore requests from noncustodial parents, even when they have said that they would be responsive. Since there is no precedent for dealing with a noncustodial parent, doing nothing is often the easiest alternative. "Treated like a nonperson" . . . "It's like I don't exist." These are common responses from noncustodial parents when discussing school. While doing nothing may appear to be a safe alternative, it may inadvertently ally the school with the custodial parent, as Mrs. Brophy's situation illustrates. Mrs. Brophy, a custodial parent, asked to be informed if her ex-husband contacted the school. Mrs. Brophy was angry at her ex-husband and felt he should not be entitled to information unless she approved. The school administrator promised her that he would certainly contact her if the ex-husband requested information. This put the school in the middle and in an alliance with Mrs. Brophy—a position it should not have to occupy.

There is a standard clause in the majority of divorce decrees making the custodial parent responsible for informing the noncustodial parent about the child's education, among other things. This does not mean that the noncustodial parent is not entitled to receive the information directly from the school (unless there's a court order stating so). It simply means that the custodial parent cannot keep these matters a secret from the other parent. "There seems to be a stereotype of what a divorce is like," says one father, "that it's the wicked parent versus the good parent in regard to who gets custody. The fact that one parent is designated 'custodial' doesn't cut the other parent out of the children's lives. I pay for their rent, food—for the school to act as though I don't exist flies in the face of reality." (As stated in chapter 1, it is estimated that in 80 to 90 percent of divorce cases, custody is not contested.)

Reality for the school, however, might well be that the noncustodial parent does not exist. The responsibilities and readjustments confronting custodial parents and the fact that they neglect to inform the school of separation and divorce at least 50 percent of the time were discussed in chapter 2. Even when custodial parents do inform the school, they seldom initiate mentioning the whereabouts and the involvement of the noncustodial parent. Noncustodial parents, on the other hand, rarely inform the school. This, too, is understandable, for they are reordering their living situation and are often steeped in other immediate concerns involving their children, such as visitation. "When you're in the process of splitting, you've got so damn much on your mind," recalled a noncustodial father. "It's hard to think of everything. In fact, at that point, I had all I could do to keep myself moving. While I was concerned about my children, I couldn't think very well. Advising the school was my last thought." Another father, who telephones his daughters daily, concurs: "I had no thought of contacting the school at the time we separated. I *believe* my ex called and told them to take it easy on the kids. When you're having your own troubles, you don't look for others."

One of the "troubles" that noncustodial parents often experience is a feeling of guilt. "The initial stage of divorce is an enormous guilt trip, and you feel if the kid screws up in school, it's your fault," concedes Mr. Jones. "My kids took it really bad. They were the first kids on their block." This feeling of guilt was related by the father who abandoned his children: "If I'd been involved more because the school had asked me, I might have made a better effort and it might have turned out better. At least you could feel you did everything you could have done if you made the effort."

The feeling of being psychologically removed—of being peripheral—is another emotion common to noncustodial parents. One father, fondly recalling that he made breakfast for his children every morning, bathed them when they were small, and tucked them in bed every night, confided, "I feel out of it. I feel so very cheated about not having my own kids. To cut that off was a very hard thing." Another father expresses this sentiment: "I feel left out—especially when I go to Open House at school with my new wife and hear about her kids. Then I think about my own kids. I feel like I've missed a lot of their upbringing."

The school enjoys a unique relationship with a child's mother and father. Its prime objective is to promote the child's personal and academic development—a goal it shares with both parents. Separation and divorce do not necessarily signal a forfeiture of these goals by the child's mother and father or by the school. Yet in practice, the majority of the time, the noncustodial parent is either dependent on the custodial parent for all school information, dependent on his children for all school information, or automatically severed from the educational aspect of his child's life.

Is it not legitimate for the school to include the noncustodial parent in his child's education, at least to some extent? Psychiatrists, lawyers, and many custodial mothers see good reason for this. "Sunday fathers are psychological criminals of the worst order," according to one suburban psychiatrist, who observes, "They make no rules; they buy affection." He suggests, "Maybe on Sunday, instead of taking the child to the zoo, the father could suggest: 'Bring your math homework and I'll help you.' " This would be a meaningful way for a father and child to spend time together. But how can a father who knows little about his child's academic program be expected to make such an offer? He can't, unless he knows which classes his child is taking and how the child is doing in those classes. The school is in a position to provide this basic, objective information by sending the noncustodial parent an invitation to Open House (or Back-to-School Night) and by sending copies of each report card.

Matrimonial lawyers agree that every noncustodial parent who is legally entitled should receive a copy of his child's report card. They see this as being in the best interest of the child. The noncustodial parent would feel less shut out, realizing that he *is* recognized as a parent. Further, his general interest in his child might be stimulated. These lawyers reason that if the child has no problems, there should be no problem with the noncustodial parent's receiving a copy of the report card. If there is a problem, they believe a responsible noncustodial parent should be aware and find out the cause. Knowing how his child is doing on a regular basis could prevent some of the resentment that results when the noncustodial parent is called in at a crisis point to try to save the child (this happens in both academic and disciplinary matters). The story of Alice and Paul is a case in point.

Alice and Paul, both well-educated professionals, had been divorced for several years. Their son, Jimmy, was eleven years old. Jimmy was having academic difficulty in school, but his father, a professional writer, wasn't aware of it. Jimmy had been diagnosed as having dyslexia (learning disabilities), and Alice was advised to take him out of the public school and enroll him in a private school reputed to have an excellent program for students with learning disabilities. The private school cost money, and Paul was asked to pay the tuition. This was how Paul learned about Jimmy's dyslexia. Until then Paul had assumed that Jimmy was doing OK in school. He hadn't been informed about the learning disability; he hadn't been consulted about private school; he didn't even understand what learning disabilities were. Paul resented having been shut out. What Jimmy really needed, he determined, was close attention from a caring person with a strong background in English. Paul suggested that Jimmy come and spend the summer with him. He would tutor Jimmy; he'd straighten out Jimmy's problems.

Alice had endured all of the headaches and emotional demands generated by Jimmy's problems. She resented his father's wanting to come in and take charge after she had gone through so much. Nevertheless, Jimmy spent the summer with his dad. And it was an ordeal for both of them. Paul had no skills for teaching a learning-disabled child; Jimmy couldn't learn. Frustration and anger surfaced.

One result of the summer's experience was a retesting of Jimmy by a reputable agency. The results were the same, but Paul's reaction was different. The agency psychologist conferred with Alice and Paul; private school was recommended. So Jimmy did attend private school that fall, with his father's approval and financial contribution.

Alice's lawyer believes that the frustration and anger produced by this experience could have been diminished (if not prevented) if

Paul had known about Jimmy's school progress in the first place. If Jimmy's school had automatically sent report cards to noncustodial parents, Paul would have been alerted to the situation by objective data (the report card), as opposed to receiving information from Jimmy's mother, whom Paul considered subjective and sometimes manipulative.

While some custodial mothers enjoy the power that goes with disseminating school and other kinds of information to their children's father, other mothers prefer that objective school data go directly from the school to the noncustodial father. These mothers favor having schools automatically send a duplicate report card to fathers. Here is the rationale: If the child is doing well in school, the father will see this and will think that the mother is doing a good job with the child. If the child is doing poorly, the father will wonder why. And although he may be inclined to blame the mother, it then gives the mother a chance to make the father feel that he, too, shoulders some of this responsibility—that she alone should not have responsibility for everything the child does or does not do.

Some mothers are very pragmatic when it comes to involving the father. "If you don't involve the father, he's not going to put his hand in his pocket—ever," reasons one divorced woman, who is thinking about present needs but is also anticipating her oldest child's going to college in three years.

If the father is responsible for contributing to his child's college expenses, it is both appropriate and sensible to involve him through more than report-card mailings and Open House invitations at the high school level. He should be included in the entire college planning process. Knowing how and why certain colleges are given consideration can do much toward alleviating one source of friction: a defensiveness on the part of fathers who understandably want to protect themselves from incurring large tuition, room, and board costs when they think that a less expensive college would be equally suitable.

Even the most caring father may feel suspicious and reluctant about being included in the college selection process if this inclusion occurs in a vacuum. One such father, who came to his daughter's college planning conference at her insistence, but who had attended no other school functions in the six years since the divorce, points out, "The father who's paying may not want to sit in a college planning conference with his ex-wife, who wants a more expensive college, while the father feels he can only pay so much."

Custodial mothers will often say privately to counselors something like, "He only wants state colleges because they're cheaper, but Sally is definitely Ivy League material. Will you talk him out of the state colleges?" One counselor's uniform response is that she will explore all colleges—state-run and private—with the father. He will then know all of the options. This counselor reports that she has yet to see a father deny his child the right to apply to a prestigious private college as long as the child is also applying to the less expensive state-run college. Further, if the child is accepted by the prestigious private college, she has never seen a father who doesn't do everything in his power to make that kind of education available to his child. The father quoted above is, in fact, sending his daughter to an expensive, prestigious eastern college. But he carefully explored the offerings at the state university before he felt comfortable paying for a private college that was more in keeping with his daughter's talents and interests.

When conferring with noncustodial parents, school professionals need to be aware of the kinds of feelings that these parents may have. They should also be aware of the great effort that may have been made by the noncustodial parent in coming to the school in the first place. Some noncustodial parents travel great distances, only to be turned away by school officials who don't know what their responsibility is or to whom they are responsible. Some noncustodial parents feel awkward and uncomfortable just entering their child's school to meet with the principal or teacher, only to be kept waiting for a meeting they have long anticipated. While school professionals may be unaccustomed to having contact with noncustodial parents, it would appear that if the parent shows interest, the school professional has an obligation to respond by giving objective information and by avoiding the temptation to make judgments.

There are sound reasons, then, for informing the noncustodial parent about his child's educational progress:

1. It recognizes his legal right to be involved—unless there's a court order to the contrary.
2. It allows the noncustodial parent to feel, and to be, more in touch with important events in his child's life, thus helping to alleviate his feeling of being psychologically removed.
3. It legitimizes the noncustodial parent's position as a parent, furthering his sense of responsibility and involvement.

The noncustodial parent is an additional resource. Does it make sense not to include him?

11

The Mechanics of Acknowledging Divorce

PROVIDING school professionals with accurate family data is often a hit-or-miss proposition. Even the most advantaged and best-run school districts admit to having shortcomings in this area. There is certain information that must be elicited accurately in the first place. Then it becomes a matter of discreetly transmitting the information to appropriate school professionals. But the responsibility doesn't end here. There must be provisions for updating information when family changes occur. And school professionals need this information to work more effectively with their students and to ensure that both parents receive notification, when appropriate, of matters in which parental involvement is expected and/or encouraged.

Unless the school obtains accurate information at the outset, there is no way of being certain of a student's family situation. There is also no way of knowing who is living in the household. The priority, therefore, is to structure a registration form that will produce this information. Forms will vary according to the needs of individual school districts, but inclusion of the following lines, designated by an asterisk (*) in figure 1, will provide the desired data. (Note that the address information must precede "With whom does student live at above address?")

Upon receiving the completed registration form in the elementary school, a class list that includes parents' names should be compiled

Figure 1

<u>REGISTRATION FORM</u>

1. Student's Name...................................Telephone...........
            Last   First   Middle

2. Address..

3. Date of Birth..............Evidence..................................

4. With whom does student live at above address:

   ....Mother

   ....Father

   ....Other Adult (s) ....
                          Specify name and relationship - e.g., aunt,
                          stepfather, etc.

5. Name of mother.........................Occupation.....................

   Address if different from line 2.......................................

   Employed by............................Business phone.................

6. Name of father.........................Occupation.....................

   Address if different from line 2.......................................

   Employed by............................Business phone.................

7. Name of stepparent or guardian if living with student:

   ....Occupation.....................

   Employed by............................Business phone.................

8. Names of other children in family.....................................

9. Date of entrance..............Last school attended....................

   Address..

10. Assigned to..................Teacher.................Grade...........

Figure 2

Pupil	Parents	(implied marital status)
Jones, Jeff	a. Mr. and Mrs. Charles Jones	Married biological parents
	b. Mrs. Ann Jones, Mr. Charles Jones	Ann Jones has custody
	c. Mrs. Ann Carnegie, Mr. Charles Jones	Mother has remarried, has custody
	d. Mr. Charles Jones, Mrs. Ann Jones	Charles Jones has custody
	e. Mrs. Ann Jones and Mr. Charles Jones	Joint custody

for each classroom teacher, as shown in figure 2. If, for example, Jeff Jones lives with both biological parents, choice (a) would be the appropriate way of listing his parents. If Jeff's mother has custody, her name would precede Jeff's father's name, and the proper designation would be (b) if she has not remarried or (c) if she has remarried or resumed her maiden name. (If this kind of information had been available, the experience of Jeff Jones, recounted on page 31, would have been avoided.)

In junior and senior high school, this same information should be obtained at the time of registration. If students are tracked or if they travel from class to class in a relatively stable group, class lists can be compiled in a central office and distributed to teachers rather easily. If, on the other hand, students follow individualized schedules that preclude moving in discernible groups, information can be made available in two ways:

1. The information can be disseminated through an alphabetical student listing that contains pertinent data for each student

Figure 3

SAMPLE: ALPHABETICAL LISTING OF STUDENTS

Student	Parents	Address	Telephone	Birth	Class	Home-room
Abbe, Adam	Mr. and Mrs. Drew Abbe	22 Bee Lane	324-7656	6/3/69	'87	234
Adis, Joe	Mrs. Sue Ray, Mr. Joe Adis	1 Ross Road	223-6898	9/1/68	'86	101

(see sample listing, figure 3). This alphabetical listing would be available to all professional staff members.

2. Teachers would be responsible for collecting these data. They would tell their students, as soon as classes stabilized at the beginning of the term, why parental information is helpful. They would then explain ways of designating parental status, and students would be asked to write the appropriate parental designation opposite their names. If Jeff Jones lived with his custodial father, for example, he would write, "Jeff Jones—Mr. Charles Jones, Mrs. Ann Jones," on a piece of paper that he would give to the teacher. Gathering information in this way respects the students' privacy. Yet it is time-consuming for teachers, who must then compile their own lists from the pieces of paper submitted by the students. Some teachers pass out index cards, which are kept in a file box. This facilitates information gathering without the teacher's having to spend time assembling a new class list.

The availability of this family data in a uniform format should be helpful in preventing embarrassing situations and in creating an awareness of students' needs. Custody is clarified, and the mother's surname is apparent at the outset. Additional family information, if school professionals have need of it, is available on the registration form or on the student update form, issued at the beginning of each school year.

The yearly update is important. Parents report that summer camps ask for a yearly update on family data, even when the child attended camp the previous summer. Having current knowledge of

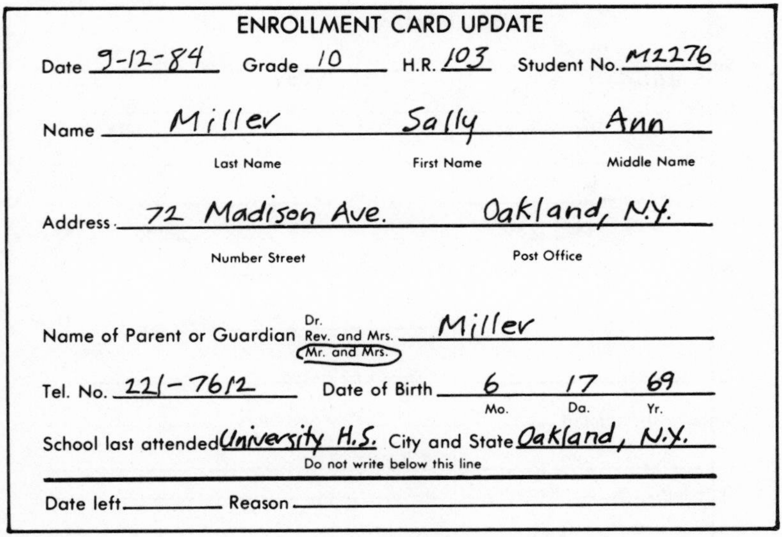

ENROLLMENT CARD UPDATE

Date 9-12-84 Grade 10 H.R. 103 Student No. M2276

Name Miller Sally Ann
Last Name First Name Middle Name

Address 72 Madison Ave. Oakland, N.Y.
Number Street Post Office

Name of Parent or Guardian Dr. / Rev. and Mrs. / (Mr. and Mrs.) Miller

Tel. No. 221-7612 Date of Birth 6 17 69
Mo. Da. Yr.

School last attended University H.S. City and State Oakland, N.Y.

Do not write below this line

Date left ______ Reason ______

Figure 4

family events—births, deaths, separation, divorce, a new person moving into the household—is as important to school professionals as having up-to-date addresses and phone numbers. School districts often ask for this information, yet haphazard methods of gathering the information and ambiguity in the forms prevail. This leads to confusion and misunderstanding for both the person filling out the update form and the person utilizing the information. Figure 4 is a *poor* example of an update form, filled out by high school students at the beginning of each school year.

An intelligent, high-achieving fifteen-year-old, whose parents divorced when she was five and whose father died when she was eleven, filled out her update form as shown in the preceding example. Circling "Mr. and Mrs." was convenient for Sally, who was sensitive about not having a father. In the same high school a more assertive girl, living with her actively feminist mother, crossed out "Mr. and Mrs." and added "Ms." Without a carefully structured form, personal interpretation, misinterpretation, and convenient omissions become significant factors. It is therefore recommended

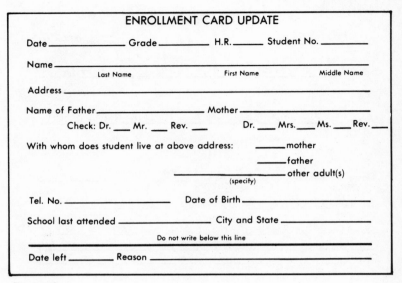

Figure 5

that an update form similar to the one shown in figure 5 be filled
out by elementary school parents and by secondary school students
at the beginning of each school year. Accurate, current information
provides at least a general idea about a student's family situation.
Specific suggestions for teachers in chapter 5 provide guidelines for
making good use of this information.

On certain occasions both divorced parents may want to be present. Parent-teacher conferences, Open House or Back-to-School
Night, and milestone events (graduation, awards assemblies) are
such occasions. Teachers, indeed school districts, are often unclear
as to how they can best meet the needs of nontraditional families at
such times. As pointed out in chapter 5, teachers should expect
from one to four parents on these occasions. While biological parents have the legal right to be present, stepparents may also have a
sincere interest in the well-being of their stepchildren.

Parent-teacher conferences offer mutual benefits. And making
the effort and the time to meet individually with each parent, if
necessary, will often be in the child's best interest. Evening meetings

for working parents may have to be built into the teacher's already busy schedule. (Guidelines can be worked out so that one day every term teachers come to work so many hours later than usual and stay in school for late-afternoon and evening parent conferences.) These parent conferences may prevent the kinds of problems and misunderstandings described in chapter 8. In addition, exchanging information and spending time with the person known as "my teacher" or "my mother" or "my father" bring added meaning to the child's discussions about family and school.

The importance of the teacher's observations in helping the single parent was discussed in chapter 3. The importance of involving the noncustodial parent was stressed in chapter 10. In order to be most helpful and avoid getting "caught in the middle" during these parent conferences, the advice of a junior high school counselor should be heeded: "Don't be judgmental. Imagine that you are a camera. Describe actions and dialogue. This puts the responsibility on the parent to think about what the teacher has said and to respond."

Since the noncustodial parent may be important in the child's life but often feels peripheral in school matters, schools should activate the machinery to make him or her feel included—assuming that he or she is legally entitled. As mentioned in chapter 10, mailing duplicate announcements of important school events and mailing duplicate report cards are two ways of accomplishing this. Noncustodial parent participation at school, it should be remembered, is often highly valued by children. In one family the children (ages seven, nine, and eleven) begged each parent to go to Open House. "If Daddy hadn't gone, he wouldn't have seen their work or met their teacher," explained the separated wife. "This is continuity in their lives, even though ours have gone in separate directions."

Making tickets available to all parents (biological parents and stepparents) for milestone events when limited tickets are the norm is as high a priority for children as it is for their parents. High school seniors with divorced, remarried parents confront the same dilemma each year: when they are alloted two graduation tickets, how do they choose between their noncustodial parent and a stepparent whom they have grown to love? One senior, who had participated on PTA- and school-sponsored panels as a child of divorce and remarriage and who had been part of a panel entitled "Pleasures, Problems, and Pressures of Living in Alternate Family Situations," left the following note for her counselor:

6/5

>Hi, Mrs. D——.
>What are the possibilities
>of me getting 2 extra graduation
>tickets?   Problems
>   Pleasures &
>   Pressures!!!
>   Thanx,
>   Diane

Diane's mother had remarried; her father had a girlfriend. She didn't want anyone to feel left out.

Schools can ease the stress by making provisions ahead of time and by informing parents and students of the procedure to follow if there are more than two parents in a child's family who wish to attend a milestone event.

The mechanics of acknowledging divorce begin, then, with the proper designation of parental status on the registration and update forms. This designation should be carried over to all forms that ask for the name of the parent or guardian. With accurate information, teachers can avoid potentially embarrassing situations, will have a more accurate picture of their students' family situations, and should be able to work more effectively and sensitively with students and their parents. By receiving duplicate mailings of report cards and important school announcements, noncustodial parents are brought into the school aspect of their children's lives. And finally, all interested parents should have the opportunity to see their child walk down the aisle on graduation day. Setting the machinery in motion should make this possible.

12
Sensitizing the Community

WHEN people are unaware of opportunities, they obviously cannot take advantage of them. And so it is with separated and divorced parents. One theme throughout this book is the difficulty these men and women experience in trying to reorder their lives. Another theme is the sensitivity they may feel about being separated or divorced. It is evidently not natural for most divorced parents to think about the school as a support system for their children, nor do they recognize the important role it can play. So the challenge is to create a community awareness of how important it is to inform the school when separation or divorce occurs. In the process of creating this awareness, the benefits to parents and to their children become obvious.

As shown in earlier chapters, custodial parents can use the school to monitor their children's adjustment and progress. They can request that their children be given teachers with appropriate personal qualities (consistency, flexibility, understanding, caring); they can request that their children have teachers who are good role models; they can ask that a special effort be made to involve their children in extracurricular activites. They can alert teachers and counselors to times when their children may need extra support or kindness; they can alert teachers to their children's special sensitivities (such as fear of abandonment or loyalty conflict).

Noncustodial parents who are legally entitled can ask for objective information about their children (such as report cards) and can ask to receive notification of important events such as Open House.

They can also join the PTA if they wish to receive its notices and publications, and they can request meetings with teachers.

Making parents aware of the benefits of this kind of involvement takes a concerted effort on the part of the schools, PTA groups, and community organizations. All of these groups are in a position to educate parents about the reasons for informing schools when crises such as separation and divorce occur. And they are able to impart this kind of information in an objective way before a crisis occurs. (As stated earlier, it is less threatening to read or hear about crises at a time when one is not personally involved in them. Yet in times of need, people remember enough information either to use it or to remember where to go for further information.)

School professionals will have to take the lead and let parents know that schools can be helpful to both custodial and noncustodial parents. This can be accomplished through school newsletters, meetings, and workshops. School professionals should encourage the local media to present public-interest articles and programs about divorce and the schools. Although countless articles have been written about divorce, schools are usually mentioned only in reference to low academic performance, truancy, or delinquency. The media should be encouraged to inform the public of the positive ways in which schools can interact with children of divorce and with their parents. The PTA can impart information to its members through newsletters and through informational programs. When community agencies sponsor programs about divorce (or for divorced parents, single parents, etc.), they can make audiences aware that informing the school in times of crisis is not only appropriate but beneficial to the healthy development of the children involved.

Each year over one million schoolchildren have parents who divorce, but including the school as a positive support system for these children has yet to become a part of the natural process. It makes no sense to ignore divorce in the school setting; it makes no sense to ignore the reactions it creates in the lives of the children involved. It does make sense to respond to the needs of these children—to meet their needs in the school setting.

Outside Support Groups

LOCAL churches, YW and YMCAs, and social service agencies, such as Jewish Family Services and community family counseling services, are an excellent source of support groups for divorced parents. Consult the local telephone directory as the need arises, then telephone. This is the only sure way to find out which organizations currently sponsor groups. (Groups form and dissolve with such regularity that last year's information may be obsolete.) The following organizations have national memberships and, to date, have stood the test of time.

Mothers Without Custody, Inc.
PO Box 602
Greenbelt, MD 20770
301-552-2319

Parents Without Partners
7910 Woodmont Ave.
Washington, DC 20014
301-654-8850

Sisterhood of Single Black Mothers
1360 Fulton Street
Brooklyn, NY 11216
718-638-0413

Checklist for Teachers

1. Remember that a teacher can best help the child of divorce by being consistent in his or her approach to the child and the course material while also being flexible at times when a child clearly feels pressured.
2. Set limits so the child does not slip into manipulative behavior, using the divorce as an excuse for irresponsibility.
3. Be alert to behavior changes or evidence of problems. Notify parents when appropriate and report observations without making judgments or attempting to analyze the behavior. A parent may notice unusual behavior but attach little significance to it unless notified by a caring "other." (Parents also appreciate the phone call or message that says all is well with their child.)
4. In the classroom, work to create an atmosphere of openness and respect for nontraditional families; and provide opportunities for children to share feelings without being judged.
5. When a child does share feelings, either in class or in private, recognize and acknowledge whatever the child is feeling in an accepting way. It is not necessary to offer an opinion or a solution.
6. If a child seeks you out privately to share feelings, listen receptively, but be careful about giving advice. Often, knowing that he or she has been listened to—especially by a respected adult—is all that the child needs.
7. If a child's problems seem serious and the parent has been communicative, offer to help the parent contact trained, helping professionals (i.e., school psychologist, social worker, guidance counselor).
8. If a child appears to be experiencing great psychological pain, inform the school psychologist or counselor immediately. Do

not take on the responsibility of trying to rescue the child yourself.

9. Avoid entering into an exclusive confidentiality relationship with a child. Instead, be prepared to refer the child to a professional should he or she disclose disturbing personal information. Make every attempt to gain the child's approval for contacting a professional should the need arise, but if something threatening to life or limb is disclosed, a professional should be contacted—with or without the child's permission.

10. Avoid becoming overattached to a youngster in crisis. Remember that your job is to offer support in difficult situations, but not to hold onto the child beyond what the child needs.

11. Should you experience a strong emotional feeling or overly identify with the child's pain, be forewarned that you may be overinvolved. Much as you may want to help, you will be unable to give the child the necessary objectivity if you are overinvolved.

12. Once a crisis has passed, continue to check in with the child on a regular basis, to "structure compassion" so that it is ongoing without being intrusive.

Checklist for Parents

1. As soon as possible, inform the school of a separation or divorce so that school personnel can be made aware of your child's needs.

2. Clarify whether or not you wish information about the family situation to be disseminated to teachers. Make it clear that while you wish school personnel to be on the lookout for problems, you do not want teachers to look for problems or treat your child differently.

3. Ask to be contacted if a teacher observes any changes in behavior or any problems.

4. If your child is in elementary school, you may want to discuss options for classroom placement, stressing the personal qualities of the teacher in meeting your child's specific needs.

5. If a teacher reports behavior such as bullying, attention seeking, stealing, regression, restlessness, daydreaming, or fantasizing, remember that these behaviors often represent attempts by the child to cope with and master psychological pain. Try to see these behaviors as distress signals; consult with the school psychologist as to ways you can be of help to (or if the behaviors continue too long, get help for) your child.

6. Cutting and truancy are common signs of distress to which school personnel may alert you. Facing normal, everyday expectations is sometimes very difficult for children under stress. Work with your child and the school counselor to confront and solve the problem. Know that options exist (e.g., weekly academic progress reports, daily attendance checks) within the framework of the school structure to provide you with information and your child with extra support during this period of adjustment.

7. Reading can often ease the burden of painful feelings as well as provide healthy strategies for coping with a crisis. Reading a book with your child can provide opportunity for excellent discussions. The librarian in your school or public library can suggest appropriate books.

8. The noncustodial parent has the right to be informed of his or her child's progress in school unless a court order prohibits release of this information. According to the research, having two interested parents seems to improve a child's school achievement as well as general adjustment.

9. While school personnel can provide helpful, objective information to both parents, they also worry about becoming "middlemen" in situations where communication between ex-spouses is poor. For school personnel to be most effective, then, try to keep them out of the middle.

Checklist for Administrators and Counselors

1. Remember that teachers want to know about their students' family circumstances because it helps them work more effectively with their students. Try to obtain the parents' permission to share this information with teachers.

2. Once a parent has informed you about a separation or divorce, arrange a meeting to ask the necessary questions (see p. 9). Let the parent know at the outset why these questions are being asked.

3. At the first meeting, elicit only the information that a parent comfortably offers, leaving the door open for future communication.

4. Respond to the parent with a nonjudgmental, caring attitude, focusing on the child's needs within the school setting.

5. Be prepared to discuss options for classroom placement, recognizing that children of divorce may need structure, consistency, and flexibility more than other children. Some teachers may be better able to meet these needs than others.

6. Make a specific appointment for a second conference or telephone conversation to follow up on the child's progress. Convey a message of availability.

7. Be alert to behavior changes brought to your attention by teachers and inform the child's parent(s) when appropriate. If you are unable to provide necessary counseling, refer the family to a qualified professional in the school or community.

8. Be aware of how difficult it may be for a parent to communicate with the school. These are tender times.

Annotated Bibliography

LIBRARIANS at school and public libraries are in
the best position to provide the most up-to-date guidance on appropriate books for children and adults. It must be remembered, however, that some people love to read; others don't. Similarly, some
people who are dealing with crises (who may or may not enjoy
reading in their spare time) will gravitate toward books for advice
and help; others purposely avoid them. The following annotated
bibliography should be especially helpful to people who are dealing
with separation and divorce.

BOOKS FOR CHILDREN: Fiction

Blume, Judy. *It's Not the End of the World*. Scarsdale, N.Y.: Brad-
bury, 1972. 169 pp. Ages 8–12. Also available in
paperback—Bantam; Braille—Library of Congress.

This is one of the books kids like best, according to one librarian. It's about
twelve-year-old Karen (the story's main character), her fourteen-year-old
brother, Jeff, and her six-year-old sister, Amy, and their reactions to their
parents' decision to separate. Shame, anger, fear, worry, and an effort to
reunite the parents are components of this realistic story. The parents are
not good examples of how parents should relate to their children in times
of stress and do not communicate well or try to explain the situation.
Eventually, the children do come to terms with the fact that divorce is
inevitable, changes will come, and one feels that "it's not the end of the
world."

Danziger, Paula. *The Divorce Express,* New York: Delacorte, 1982. 144 pp. Ages 10–14. Also available in paperback—Dell.

A favorite author for this age group writes about Phoebe Brooks, a ninth-grader whose parents have joint custody. Phoebe lives in Woodstock, New York, during the week with her father and takes the bus to New York City every weekend to be with her mother. Children in similar family situations take the bus, the "Divorce Express," with Phoebe, including her best friend, whose parents are also divorced. Phoebe's anger about the divorce, her adjustments to change (new school, new friends, mother's boyfriend and imminent marriage), and her attempts to cope and understand ("Protecting parents' feelings can be a full-time job") are issues that many young people will identify with.

Goff, Beth. *Where Is Daddy? The Story of a Divorce.* Boston: Beacon, 1969. 32 pp. Ages 4–8. Also available in Large Print.

This award-winning story about little Janey's reaction to her parents' divorce has been helpful to divorcing parents and young children for over fifteen years. Anger, fear of abandonment, feelings of guilt, and confusion are experienced as Janey tries to understand what is happening. At breakfast one morning, Janey's father is absent. When she asks "Where's Daddy?" her mother says that he has left; then Janey asks when he's coming back and her mother says she isn't certain. Janey wonders if he has left because he is angry at her. He returns to take her to the beach one day and during their time together explains that he and her mother are getting a divorce. Janey, her mother, and her dog, Funny, move in with Janey's grandmother. The routines are different; her grandmother scolds her because she yells a lot and tells her that if she acts bad her mother, who has taken a job, won't want to come home. So Janey represses her feelings, worrying that her mother will leave her as her father did. Ultimately her mother recognizes Janey's insecurity and reassures her; the grandmother becomes more patient; her father visits; and Janey begins to feel more secure.

Helmering, Doris. *I Have Two Families.* Nashville, Tenn.: Abingdon, 1981. 48 pp. Ages 6–8.

This short, easy-to-understand book addresses the adjustments and concerns of young children in joint-custody situations. Eight-year-old Patty and her younger brother, Michael, are scared and wonder what will happen to them when their parents divorce. Both parents decide that the children will live primarily with their father, but spend Wednesday nights and Sundays at their mother's house. Patty relates how happy she is that she didn't "have to choose between Mom and Dad." The different routines and expectations in each household seem to be taken in stride, but Patty confesses that it's a pain "when you want to ride your bicycle and your bicycle is at the other house." The story is optimistic, yet realistic.

Mann, Peggy. *My Dad Lives in a Downtown Hotel*. New York: Doubleday, 1973. 92 pp. Ages 8–11. Also available in paperback—Avon.

Joey is accustomed to his parents fighting "nice and soft," but one night there is a bad fight, the front door slams shut, and Joey's father leaves. The next morning Joey's mother tells him that his father is not going to live with them anymore. Intense anger, sadness, guilt, and an unsuccessful plan to get his father to return home are followed by acceptance. Joey's parents let him know that they both love him very much, and he sees his father, who now lives in a hotel, more often than he ever did. Finally, an older boy whose father lives elsewhere helps Joey to realize that he's not alone. This book has been popular for many years.

Miles, Betty. *The Trouble with Thirteen*. New York: Knopf, 1979. 108 pp. Ages 9–12. Also available in paperback—Avon.

This is a story about friendship and about change. Although divorce is not the central theme, the book provides young people with a good example of how to respond to a friend whose parents have just revealed their intention to divorce. Annie and Rachel, twelve years old, are best friends, and at the beginning of the book life is perfect for them. Then comes the impending divorce of Rachel's parents, the death of Annie's beloved dog, and the news that Rachel will soon be moving. Many youngsters wonder what they should say to—and how they should act with—friends whose parents are divorcing. This realistic story can provide them with guidance.

Newfield, Marcia. *A Book for Jodan*. New York: Atheneum, 1975.
  48 pp. Ages 7–11.

Jodan has a special loving relationship with both of her parents, and their decision to divorce necessitates Jodan's moving with her mother to California—a long way from Massachusetts, where her father remains in the family home. Jodan greatly misses her father; wonders why her parents can't get back together; and finally visits her father during a vacation. In this very poignant segment, Jodan's father shows his love and concern by giving her a special scrapbook he has made for her, a scrapbook she can take back to California to be reminded of his caring, his love, his philosophy, his optimism for the future.

Okimoto, Jean Davies. *My Mother Is Not Married to My Father*.
  New York: Pocket Books/Archway Paperback,
  1979. 103 pp. Ages 9–13.

While their father is away on one of his many business trips, Cynthia, age eleven, and Sara, age six, learn from their mother that their parents are going to divorce. Denial, anger, fear of abandonment, sadness, regression, confusion, and guilt are presented realistically and responsibly through thoughts ("One of the crummy things about divorces is that there are so many changes that it really makes a person worry if anything will be the same—mostly if the parents will still love you. Even if they don't love each other") and conversations—often with the family's cat, Martha ("If parents decide to get divorced, there's nothing kids can do about it. . . . It's not fair!"). Being spoiled on weekends with their dad, jealousy toward their father's girlfriend, adjustment to their mother's efforts to cope and to her dating, and the issue of relationships with stepparents and stepsiblings are presented in this story set in Washington State. This book is a favorite with preadolescents in one suburban New York library and portrays—often with humor—common problems and sound ways of coping.

Simon, Norma. *I Wish I Had My Father*. Niles, Ill.: Whitman,
  1983. 32 pp. Ages 6–9 and teachers.

A young boy whose parents divorced no longer sees his father. When the teacher suggests making something for Father's Day, his feelings and those of his friend Grace (also fatherless) are presented. The author states: "This book can begin to help adults and children find words to express the thoughts, memories, emotions, and expectations that surround the significant, though absent, parent in the children's life." Obviously, adults can make the absence of a parent somewhat easier for children, and while this book is written for children, it offers insights to which adults—especially school professionals—should be sensitive.

Stolz, Mary. *Leap before You Look.* New York: Harper & Row, 1972. 259 pp. Ages 12–16. Also available in paperback—Dell.

Living in a home where her parents seem "beleaguered" and parental friction is commonplace, fourteen-year-old Jimmie is nevertheless initially unable to accept her parents' decision to divorce. The anger, the concern about being cared for, the sadness, the hurt, the need to make sense out of the situation—these feelings and concerns are set against the background of normal adolescent problems. Jimmie is bright and perceptive and has good support from her girlfriends, one of whom has a several-times-married mother. Jimmie begins to examine her feelings about each member of her family (including grandmothers), and at the story's end we know that she is getting on with her life. This book, set against the background of the early seventies, has retained its popularity and is worth reading for the insights offered.

Books for Children: Nonfiction

Arnold, William V. *When Your Parents Divorce.* Philadelphia: Westminster, 1980. 116 pp. Ages teens–young adults.

This nonfiction paperback book is written by a Presbyterian minister and is based on his experiences counseling people in the middle of separation and divorce. Although part of a "Christian Care Books" series, it is appropriate for teenagers and young adults whether or not they have a religious orientation. Writing in an informal, personal style, Arnold explains the feelings, thoughts, and behavior commonly experienced by teenagers and young adults whose parents divorce. He gives some advice (e.g., "Use their [your parents'] experience as an education for yourself. It's an education that teaches you to be very careful about choosing a spouse"), encouraging young people to assess their feelings, thoughts, and needs so that they will develop healthy relationships during their lives. This book fills a void in helpful divorce literature for this age group. It contains real substance in relatively few pages and is quick, easy reading.

Gardner, Richard. *The Boys' and Girls' Book about Divorce*. New York: Jason Aronson, 1970. 159 pp. Ages 7–14. Also available in paperback—Bantam; Braille—Library of Congress.

In a straighforward manner, child psychiatrist Richard Gardner discusses issues of concern to children whose parents have divorced. Topics such as "Who's to Blame," "How to Find Out If Someone Loves You," "Anger," "The Fear of Being Left Alone," as well as how to get along better with your divorced mother and father, your stepmother and stepfather, and a chapter entitled "If You Have to See a Therapist," make this book probably as complete a treatment of divorce as it affects young children as this age group can handle. There is an important introduction for parents; indeed, parents will find this book helpful in gaining insights into their children's concerns. One high school counselor has lent her Gardner book to high school students for use with their younger brothers and sisters. This is one way of providing support to younger siblings experiencing divorce. At the same time the teenagers experience a feeling of worth, develop a closer relationship with the younger siblings, and acquire an increased understanding of family dynamics.

Glass, Stuart M. *A Divorce Dictionary: A Book for You and Your Children*. Boston: Little Brown, 1979. 71 pp. New York: Four Winds, 1980. Ages 7–12.

Beginning alphabetically with "abandonment" and continuing through "visitation rights," this dictionary defines terms that children encounter during the divorce process. Based on his teaching of divorce as a legal proceeding, to children in junior high and high school, attorney Glass presents legal definitions in language children can understand—using anecdotes and a question-and-answer format. Complicated terminology is made simple; the dictionary is easy to use. A good resource book!

LeShan, Eda. *What's Going to Happen to Me? When Parents Separate or Divorce.* New York: Four Winds, 1978. 134 pp. Ages 8 up.

Using examples and anecdotes from real life, Eda LeShan, a family counselor and well-known author, helps children understand the feelings and cope with the problems caused by separation and divorce. She discusses and legitimizes children's feelings, explains how they may change along the continuum of the family's experience, encourages frank parent-child communication, and explains how parents are also suffering during this period and how they may use their children in inappropriate ways (e.g., as go-betweens). The importance of supportive people outside the family is stressed, as well as acceptance of the divorce and adjustment to a parent's remarriage and to stepsiblings. Sound advice is given in a friendly manner. This nonfiction book is highly recommended by many professionals.

Richards, Arlene, and Willis, Irene. *How to Get It Together When Your Parents Are Coming Apart.* New York: McKay, 1976. 170 pp. Ages 12–18. Also available in paperback—Bantam.

Using a multitude of short anecdotes to illustrate the variety of experiences that teenagers may encounter, Richards and Willis have written a helpful book covering chronologically the road to and through divorce. Factors that may lead to the decision to divorce, problem parents, their effect on the family and ways that teenagers can respond constructively to their problems, what happens during divorce legally and emotionally to children and parents, as well as problems readjusting to the new family situation are presented.

Rofes, Eric, editor. *The Kids' Book of Divorce: By, for and about Kids.* Lexington, Mass.: Lewis, 1981. 144 pp. Ages 8–13. Also available in paperback—Vintage.

Twenty students, fourteen of whom have divorced parents, wrote this book under the supervision of their twenty-six-year-old teacher, Mr. Rofes. These children, aged eleven to fourteen, were part of The Unit, a class at the private Fayerweather Street School, in Cambridge, Mass. The students, after meeting in discussion groups, read fiction and nonfiction books on divorce. Some important issues weren't addressed, they said, and they felt some of the adult authors talked down to kids. The result is this book, written from the kids' point of view, reflecting a broader picture of the divorce experience. The chapter "Separation: It's Not the End of the World" addresses chronologically parents' and children's feelings and the legal concerns that come up during this period. The contents of a separation agreement are explained as they relate to a hypothetical child, Caleb, giving valuable information and suggestions to children. Chapters include: "The Legal Issues," "The First Legal Day of Divorce," "Weekend Santa," "Stepparents and Other People" among others. Youngsters should easily identify with the content and find this book helpful.

Simon, Norma. *All Kinds of Families.* Niles, Ill.: Whitman, 1976. 36 pp. Ages 5–7 and teachers.

This book's purpose is to legitimize family differences to young children and let children know that they belong to a family and that is special. Big families, small families, fatherless and motherless and childless families as well as other variations on the theme are presented through verse and pictures. This book can stimulate the kind of project suggested in chapter 5, p. 35.

BOOKS FOR PARENTS: Nonfiction

Francke, Linda Bird. *Growing up Divorced.* New York: Linden Press/Simon & Schuster, 1983. 303 pp. Also available in paperback—Fawcett.

In one of the most complete treatments of children's reactions to divorce, Ms. Francke draws upon findings of current researchers (Wallerstein and Kelly, Hetherington, and Cox and Cox among others) as well as her own. Children's experiences and feelings are presented in separate chapters by stages (infancy, preschoolers, children 6–8, children 9–12, teenagers), making this an easy-to-use reference book. "How Parents Can Help" sections are included at the end of each chapter. Ms. Francke has also included a chapter on divorce and the schools.

Gardner, Richard A. *The Parents' Book About Divorce.* New York: Doubleday, 1977. 368 pp.

Judging from the shopworn look, weakened spine, and underlined passages, one library copy of psychiatrist Richard Gardner's book has been read by many people and justifiably so. The basic assumption of the book is that children of divorce are more likely to develop harmful psychological reactions than children growing up in an "intact, relatively secure home." Dr. Gardner presents the most common reactions and ways that parents can deal with them so that some of the psychological problems children experience because of parental "inexperience, naiveté, and misguidance" can be alleviated. Using anecdotes to stress points, he imparts a wealth of information as if he were talking informally to the reader. "Telling the Children," "Early Post-separation Adjustment," "Dealing with Children's Post-separation Problems," "Common Parental Difficulties that Contribute to Children's Post-separation Maladjustments" are some of the chapter headings. Subheadings exist within each chapter and are outlined in the Table of Contents for easy reference.

Wallerstein, Judith S., and Kelly, Joan B. *Surviving the Breakup*. New York: Basic Books, 1980. 341 pp.

Reporting on findings from their Children of Divorce Project five years postdivorce, Wallerstein and Kelly inform the reader of the initial experience of participants in the Project during parental separation (including children's experiences and responses during this period); follow up on the family members after the separation (reporting on changes in parent-child relationships, the child and the custodial parent, the visiting parent, the child's view of visiting); discuss parents and children in transition; and finally report on the five-year follow-up (in terms of how children and adolescents reflect on the divorce, how they're functioning, the father-child relationship, and children's school functioning). The research is interesting and should provide helpful insights to adults who want a better understanding of what happens as fathers, mothers, and children adjust to divorce.

Weiss, Robert S. *Marital Separation*. New York: Basic Books, 1975. 334 pp.

Robert Weiss is a sociologist and professor at the University of Massachusetts. He is also a parent who has experienced divorce. Based on material gathered from members of Parents Without Partners, as well as from studies and seminars that he has conducted, he offers a sensitive, informative, and helpful book. A multitude of true experiences enrich the theories and findings, which are presented in terms a layperson can well comprehend. Parents reading this book will realize that they are not alone in their feelings and experiences and should benefit from the information given.

BOOKS FOR TEACHERS: Nonfiction

Bernstein, Joanne E. *Books to Help Children Cope with Separation and Loss.* 2nd edition. New York: Bowker, 1983. 439 pp.

633 very complete, well-annotated bibliographies of fiction and nonfiction books, appropriate for three- to sixteen-year-olds, are presented in this 2nd edition. Also included are a discussion of and techniques for using bibliotherapy. An excellent resource.

Dreyer, Sharon S. *The Bookfinder.* Vol. 2. Circle Pines, Minn.: American Guidance Service, 1981.

This reference work is uniquely constructed—it is two books (one literally on top of the other) inside one cover. Over 450 topics are categorized in the top book according to psychological, behavioral, and developmental headings. Title and author are given in the top section, whereupon one goes to the bottom section, arranged alphabetically by author, to read the 723 annotated bibliographies appropriate for youths aged two to fifteen. This arrangement is very easy to use.

Fassler, Joan. *Helping Children Cope: Mastering Stress through Books and Stories.* New York: Free Press, 1978. 162 pp.

Written for use with youngsters four to eight, this resource book can provide a comfortable means of introducing discussions about problems and feelings. Child psychologist Fassler also describes areas of potential stress for young children, then reviews professional literature for each area as well as appropriate children's books.

Jewett, Claudia. *Helping Children Cope with Separation and Loss.* Cambridge, Mass.: Harvard University Press, 1982. 146 pp.

This book is written for elementary school teachers who want to establish a closer, more helpful relationship with children experiencing separation and loss crises.

Index